OUT-OF-BODY ADVENTURES

30 Days to the Most Exciting Experience of Your Life

RICK STACK

CONTEMPORARY
BOOKS

CHICAGO

Library of Congress Cataloging-in-Publication Data

Stack, Rick.
  Out-of-body adventures.

  I. Astral projection.   I. Title
BF1389.A7S73   1988   133.9   88-28132
ISBN 0-8092-4560-4 (pbk.)

Published by Contemporary Books, Inc.
180 North Michigan Avenue, Chicago, Illinois 60601
Manufactured in the United States of America
International Standard Book Number: 0-8092-4560-4

Published simultaneously in Canada by Beaverbooks, Ltd.
195 Allstate Parkway, Valleywood Business Park
Markham, Ontario L3R 4T8 Canada

ACKNOWLEDGMENTS

I would like to thank my wife and agent, Anne Marie O'Farrell, for her bottomless heart and limitless energy.

I would like to thank my former teachers, Jane Roberts and Seth, for their warm friendship, extraordinary sanity, and wisdom.

I would like to thank the people who graciously allowed me to use their dreams and out-of-body experiences in this book. Pseudonyms have been used for all such experiences.

I would like to thank my editor, Stacy Prince, for her humor and sharp pencils.

And I would like to thank my infant son, Cody, for waiting until the book was finished before arriving.

CONTENTS

PREFACE

This book is designed to take the study and practice of out-of-body experiences out of the realm of research laboratories and esoteric mysticism and into the living rooms and bedrooms of the world—where they belong. It provides a simple, effective approach for learning how to leave the body consciously that anyone can use. It also provides instruction on how to get the most out of your trip. Out-of-body experiences (OOBEs) are incredibly exciting, spiritually enlightening, and *easy to do*. If you are willing to start with the assumption that your current beliefs about the universe may not be the whole truth and that the universe is indeed a mystery to be explored with the same excitement and open-mindedness that any child naturally possesses, I can promise you an adventure you will never forget.

But if it's so easy to go out-of-body, why is this topic still relatively esoteric? Quite simply, people are largely unaware of their natural ability to leave the body because their belief systems do not allow for the existence of such experiences, or they consider them an idle pursuit at best. For those who do consider

OOBEs an area worthy of attention, firsthand experience is the most direct path for exploration.

Those who wish to pursue firsthand experience, however, may find that their own attitudes are the key to progress in learning how to become astral explorers. For that reason, this book provides a step-by-step procedure for creating a mental climate conducive to achieving these extraordinary journeys before presenting effective, uncomplicated techniques for actually inducing out-of-body experiences. This preliminary belief work is designed to alter certain limiting ideas and enable you to overcome fears of, or resistance to, traveling outside your physical body.

For many people, the belief work and the preliminary dream work presented herein will be a crucial element for success. How long it will take you to accomplish the preliminary work will depend on you. If you already have experience working with your dreams, you have a head start. If your belief systems are relatively positive and expansive, then the belief work required may be minimal.

After reading this book, performing the preliminary work, and starting to regularly utilize the OOBE induction techniques presented, you can reasonably expect to achieve your first OOBE within thirty days, though some may take considerably longer. Anyone can do it, but not everyone will, because some people will not agree to loosen their limiting beliefs enough to allow themselves these kinds of experiences. If you really have the desire, though, this book will provide the means.

I have had many out-of-body experiences, and they have added immeasurably to my life. I hope to communicate the importance and value of this neglected area of human potential. You can appreciate the true value of this art form, however, only when you have actually experienced being outside of your body numerous times. The object of this book, therefore, is to enable you to have not just one but many OOBEs and make them a frequent and natural part of your life. Then you will really begin to understand what they are all about.

Someday, in a more enlightened culture, the art of interdimensional travel outside of the physical body will enjoy a more prominent and respected position. Someday people will explore inner reality with the same fervor with which they have explored outer reality (i.e., the physical universe) and thus take a giant step in the evolution of humankind's understanding. As always, such advances will be accomplished by individuals whose energy and curiosity will not be quelled by fairy tales and prejudice and who insist on finding things out for themselves.

INTRODUCTION

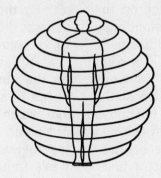

When I was a teenager, I became obsessed with understanding what existence was all about. As long as I can remember I was curious about the universe, but at a certain point in my life this curiosity became an unquenchable thirst. Finally, the urge became so strong that I just had to get some answers before continuing with what I thought of as a "normal" life.

Prior to this, I had tried to latch on to science as a possible source of understanding. It didn't take me long to become disillusioned with the scientific perspective. I'll never forget one day in Advanced Biology 1 during the first term of my senior year in high school. As the instructor unraveled some of the marvels of nature for us, I couldn't resist asking him what was the greater purpose behind what he was describing. My instructor just smiled and virtually waxed poetic as he explained that my question was teleological and therefore inappropriate for discussion. Well, I didn't know what *teleological* meant, but I was pretty disconcerted that my instructor acted as if my question wasn't even *important*. He proceeded with his lesson; I proceeded to reevaluate my plan to take Advanced Biology 2. (I finally opted for Sculpture 1, a class with a twenty-to-one ratio of female to male students—clearly a more fun way to learn about biology.)

By the time I started my junior year in college, the seeds of my discontent had grown to enormous proportions. I found the scientific explanation of how we got here to border on the absurd. To simplify it greatly: Life began in some primordial ocean a long time ago, when, *by chance*, the right combination of chemicals and elements and conditions got together, and poof—there was life. Even Darwin's impressive theory of evolution effectively eliminated the need for a higher guiding intelligence in the equation, suggesting mutations occur *by chance alone* and only the best of a species survive and thrive.

This "by-chance-alone" thing was really too much. Were these people serious? Was this really what the greatest minds of our time had come up with? Did they really believe that all the incredibly intricate and ingenious wonders of nature were accomplished without ANY form of guiding cosmic intelligence? I knew that some of the religious concepts that humankind had come up with over the years were rather childish, but this concept seemed just as naive. The scientific perspective was great for making rocket ships and toaster ovens, but when it came to deeper issues, it was turning into a big disappointment.

I began an intense and sometimes turbulent period of study. My research ran the gamut from psychology, mythology, and religion to theosophy, the gnosis, Egyptology, and the various esoteric traditions of the ages. I became involved with dreams. I learned that dreams were an incredible resource for knowledge and understanding. I learned that the dream world was a doorway to other dimensions of experience that were just as valid and important as the world I knew. I began to practice lucid dreaming, the art of becoming fully awake within the dream state and then consciously manipulating the events that occur. Yet I did not fully understand that I was preprogramming my inner experiences according to my own beliefs and expectations.

It was in 1970 that I picked up my first Seth book. Seth is the nonphysical personality and teacher who spoke through the late author Jane Roberts while she was in trance. Material communicated by Seth has been published in ten volumes to date. (See Bibliography for a list of these titles.) I was particularly impressed by Seth and in early 1972 found myself driving up to Elmira, New York, with a couple of friends at Jane Roberts's invitation to attend her weekly ESP class. Although the Seth books now have a fairly large following, at that time interest in Jane's work was just beginning, and her class consisted of about a dozen students. Jane would go into trance and "channel" Seth, who turned out to be an impressive teacher indeed.

I became a regular member of Jane's class, and I made the ten-hour round-trip drive from New York City to Elmira practically every Tuesday for several years. To say that I was affected by studying with Jane and Seth is an understatement, for as a result of that class I began to truly and deeply understand that each individual creates his or her own reality. I also learned to listen to the voice of my inner multidimensional self, where I can find as many answers as I have questions.

As my metaphysical understanding grew, I became more and more intrigued by out-of-body experiences. I was determined to advance my knowledge in this area through firsthand experience. Around the summer of 1972, I accidentally discovered a method enabling me to induce out-of-bodies with relative ease (you will learn this method in Chapter 12). My first experiences were so amazing to me that I'll never forget them.

I stretched out in an easy chair in my bedroom and gave myself some suggestions about having an out-of-body experience:

The next thing I knew I was in a park about twenty miles from my apartment. I used to play in this park as a child. I felt incredibly exhilarated and filled with energy that literally rippled through my body. There were trees and fields all around; they were somehow more vivid, more alive, more colorful than I had ever seen. It was as if I had stepped into a magical forest, glowing with aliveness. Things didn't seem just real, they seemed super real. I was vibrating with energy, feeling ecstatic, but also feeling quite disoriented. I knew where I was, but I didn't know how I got there. I had forgotten that I had just sat down to do an out-of-body. I was feeling totally tripped out, and I finally concluded that someone had slipped LSD or another drug into something I drank. I looked down and noticed that I didn't have any clothes on. I started to become concerned. I thought to myself, "Great. I'm in Alley Pond Park, I'm tripping on some strange drug, and I have no clothes on. What am I going to do? How am I going to get back home? I don't even have a token for the train." So I wandered around, vibrating, the trees glowing, strangely not too upset by my predicament. The sun was just beginning to rise, and I had not seen another soul in the park. Then as I passed a playground, I noticed a small boy playing inside. It seemed really strange because the child was very young and all alone. I walked over to the fence surrounding the playground and looked at him. There was something very odd about this kid. All of a sudden he looked me straight in the eye and said, "This universe is for you!" Instantly, I remembered my body was twenty miles away. I had just attempted to go out-of-body and had succeeded. I was out. I was overwhelmed with excitement and joy. Without thinking, I lifted up my hands to fly and took off like a rocket. I had had numerous flying dreams before, but this was something quite different. There was no way that this was just my imagination. I was flying, curving, twisting, soaring over the treetops of Alley Pond Park. My normal ego consciousness was fully present and having the ride of its life. I flew around for awhile and eventually landed on a grassy hill in the park. I felt it was time to go home. I closed my eyes, leaned back, and said, "Back to the Bronx, back to the Bronx." I felt a sensation of motion and tremendous speed. Then I found myself back in my physical body. My eyes were still closed, but I could see right through my eyelids. I was impressed! Finally, after examining my room through my eyelids for a minute or so, I opened my eyes. Things looked a little strange for awhile—as if I was not yet fully tuned in to the appropriate channel. Within a minute or two, everything solidified and returned to normal. I was back, safe and sound!

I was really blown away by the experience. I was still dissatisfied, though, because I had not yet *consciously* witnessed the actual separation from the physical, and I was determined to do so. I continued to practice my newfound technique and for awhile had out-of-body experiences about every other day. Within a couple of weeks, I lifted out of my body in my bedroom while retaining awareness of what was going on the entire time.

My body felt as if it were going to sleep.

Something weird was going on, however, because I was still fully awake. I was literally watching my body fall asleep. I could feel myself moving through the stages of sleep while retaining full consciousness. It was fascinating. I was still in my body, but I was no longer connected to it in the normal manner. I couldn't move my muscles. My eyes were closed, but I could see the room perfectly through my eyelids. Somehow I knew just what to do. I willed myself to move upward. I watched in awe as my nonphysical, or astral, leg moved out of my physical leg, and the rest of my astral body followed. I stood in the bedroom directly in front of the chair containing my physical body and proceeded to walk through the door into the next room. As usual, I was feeling tremendously energized and exhilarated. It occurred to me that I didn't need doors any more, so I walked through the wall into the living room, sat down in a chair, and went into a fit of laughter. I could hardly *believe what was happening. In that moment I knew, in a deeply intuitive way, that my existence was independent of my physical body.*

Since that time, I have had many out-of-body adventures. As my understanding of the nature of reality grew, so did the quality of my excursions outside the body. Soon I began to share my knowledge by teaching courses on OOBEs, the Seth material, dreams, and metaphysics, which I have now done for over ten years. I decided to write this book when I realized that most people found inducing OOBEs difficult and that I could offer a method that even beginners could use with relative ease.

In order to facilitate learning how to induce OOBEs, it is important to develop an understanding of metaphysics and the impact of your own attitudes. Your fundamental beliefs about how the universe works will affect both your ability to induce OOBEs and the types of experiences you will encounter. For these reasons, be sure to read the book in the order presented; do not skip ahead to the exercises until you have completed your belief work.

As mentioned, the time it will take to complete the preliminary work will vary according to the individual. When you have finished this preparatory work, proceed to the OOBE induction techniques. Plan to do them every day for a month. Again, it is reasonable to assume that you will have your first OOBE within thirty practice trials. This expectation, in fact, can help you to achieve your first OOBE. There will, however, be considerable variation here. Some people may get out after only a few trials, while others may need to keep at it for several months. If you are persistent and determined, you will succeed.

Another factor to keep in mind is your overall environment and state of mind. If your job is a stressful one, or if you are otherwise engaged in an anxiety-provoking lifestyle, it could interfere with your OOBE work. If this is the case, it may be advisable to begin working with the induction techniques during a vacation so that you can easily practice them daily in a relaxed environment. Another alternative for those who have a hectic workweek is to practice the induction techniques for fifteen consecutive weekends, which would give you thirty trials overall. While not optimal, it is an option for those who need it. If the weekend schedule doesn't produce results, you may need to create the time to practice every day for awhile in order to get the ball rolling. Once you do get going, don't stop—try to incorporate your OOBE work into your schedule on an ongoing basis.

1
SCIENCE FACT OR SCIENCE FICTION?

The belief that we all have some sort of non-physical soul is a part of most of the world's religions. Out-of-body experiences have been reported for centuries in cultures around the globe. There are numerous accounts of people who left their bodies and whose "apparitions" were subsequently seen by others. There are also numerous accounts of OOBEs in which people were able to perceive objects that were a good distance from their physical bodies; such perceptions were later verified.

Oliver Fox describes an example of such an experience in his classic work *Astral Projection: A Record of Out-of-the-Body Experiences*.[1] On a summer night in 1905 a girl-friend, Elsie, appeared in his bedroom while she was out-of-body. Earlier that day she had informed him she was going to do this. Fox, who thought he too was probably in his "astral counterpart" at the time, saw a "large egg-shaped cloud of intensely brilliant bluish-white light" with Elsie in the middle. Elsie appeared perfectly solid as she ran her fingers along Fox's desk and looked at him. The following evening Fox met with Elsie, who told him in no uncertain terms that the night before she had gone to sleep and willed herself to Fox's room. Elsie was able to accurately describe much of the room's contents, including the placement of the furniture and various objects. She even said that his desk had a gilt ridge on it, despite Fox's claim that it was a gilt line, not a ridge. She insisted that she had felt the ridge, and Fox insisted that he knew his own desk. Fox later examined the desk and discovered the ridge that Elsie had described. Fox was certain that Elsie had never been in his room while in her physical body and that he had never described to her the contents she reported seeing.

Another example comes from an individual named Carl, who has attended some of my classes and workshops. Carl had just flown into California after agreeing earlier that day to try to meet a friend that night in a dream or OOBE. His friend lived in New Jersey. At around 4:00 A.M., Carl attempted to induce an OOBE.

I heard ringing in my ears. I let it increase until it got to a certain point, and then I just lifted up out of my body. As I lifted up, I went completely into another dimension. I wasn't in the same room anymore, which confused me. At first I started thinking, "How am I going to get to New Jersey?" I tried to think of all the normal, rational ways to do it. Then I heard a voice, which said, "You don't have to do all that. Just concentrate on him and you'll find him." So I closed my eyes and concentrated, and suddenly his face appeared before me. He was sitting down with his eyes closed, as if in meditation. I was aware that I was in his room, but I couldn't see any of the surroundings. The more I concentrated on him, the more I thought that he knew that I was there. But he didn't seem to be able to turn and look at me. I kept calling out to him, "Look, I'm out-of-body, I'm in California." I was trying to make him understand. He seemed like he knew I was there, but he couldn't turn and face me. I did that for a good thirty seconds, trying to get through to him. Finally, as he opened his eyes and turned in my direction, the scene vanished, and I was back in bed in California.

So I talked to him the next day and found that he was sitting in meditation, just like I saw him, at the same time that I was out of my body. It was 7:00 A.M. where he was and 4:00 A.M. where I was. He said that he thought I would be asleep then, and he was concentrating on me.

The two main interpretations of what really happens during an OOBE are the *extrasomatic* theory and the *intrasomatic* theory. The extrasomatic theory states that during an

OOBE some significant part of the participant actually leaves the physical body and floats around somewhere outside of it. The *intrasomatic* theory states that no significant part of the participant ever leaves the physical body during an OOBE.

A popular trend in the scientific community is to explain away OOBEs in which people claim to have been at a certain location and are able to accurately describe what they saw there by saying that it is "just" ESP (extrasensory perception). But any perception realized without the use of the normal physical senses is extrasensory. Therefore, those who leave their bodies and accurately perceive a distant location must, by definition, be using ESP, whether or not some part of the personality actually leaves the body!

A notable study by Osis and McCormick involved an out-of-body subject trying to view a target that was contained within an optical image device and could be viewed only from a specific location.[2] The target was a picture composed of several elements. These elements were not physically together in any one place within the apparatus. If you looked through the viewing window from a point directly in front of the apparatus, however, the various elements of the final target came together as an optical illusion. The OOBE subject, Alex Tanous, was instructed to project into the room with the target, which was several rooms away, and to try to view it. Meanwhile, the experimenters attempted to measure physical effects at the target location (effects that may be caused by the subject's out-of-body presence). They placed sensor plates in a shielded chamber at the viewing location. The sensors were capable of picking up very small movements, or vibrations, which would then generate electrical impulses in extremely sensitive strain gauges. These strain gauges, therefore, enabled the experimenters to note very minute changes in the vibration of the sensor plates. Tanous was led to believe that the strain gauges were being used only for a subsequent task in order to reduce the possibility of his deliberately trying to affect the sensors while attempting to view the optical image device.

Osis and McCormick thought that the OOBE might be a state that fluctuated with respect to degree of externalization; that is to say, there may be degrees of clarity or intensity in the out-of-body state. It may be possible, for example, to be both partially out of and partially in your body. The investigators hypothesized that when the OOBE subject was most fully out and, consequently, able to view the target more accurately, there would be greater mechanical (physical) effect caused by the experient's out-of-body presence than there would be when the subject was less out and, therefore, less able to accurately view the target.

The results of the Osis-McCormick study supported their hypothesis "that ostensibly unintentional kinetic effects can occur as by-products of narrowly localized OB [out-of-body] vision." In other words, apparently unintentional physical motion or effects can occur when someone sees something at a specific location while feeling that he is out-of-body. The strain gauge activation level that occurred when the subject was viewing the target and scored "hits" was significantly higher than when the subject scored "misses." This finding lends some support to the concept that the greater vibration of the sensor plates was caused by some exteriorized portion of the subject's personality.

From what I understand, the scientific community currently is not rushing to follow up on studies like the above. One would think that the voluminous anecdotal material reporting OOBEs, in conjunction with studies (albeit relatively few) that lend some support to the extrasomatic theory, is reason enough for the scientific community to start waking up. This seems to be happening here and there, but at a slow pace.

One more study I would like to mention briefly was done by Morris, Harary, Janis, Hartwell, and Roll.[3] The investigators wanted to see whether an individual having an OOBE could be detected at a remote location by physical, animal, or human detectors. In one procedure, the human detectors were told that they would be visited twice by the subject while out of his body during a forty-minute period. The human detectors showed a significant tendency to respond to the subject's alleged out-of-body presence during this part of the experiment. The other procedure used with the human detectors consisted of two short periods during which the subject would visit in the out-of-body state and two control periods of equivalent length. The human detectors did not respond significantly more during OOBE periods than during control periods in this part of the experiment.

One of the animal detectors, a kitten, was significantly quieter and less active during OOBE periods than during control periods. The subject, Harary, "was instructed to 'visit' the kitten, to experience comforting and playing with it," while out of his body. The kitten was active during baseline (preliminary observation) periods and control periods but became extremely quiet during OOBE periods. The kitten meowed thirty-seven times during the eight control periods but did not vocalize at all during the OOBE periods. In a second study with the kitten, the experimenters wished to see whether it could orient toward a specific direction where Harary was visiting while out-of-body. The overall results were statistically insignificant, but one of the experimenters, who was observing the kitten, reported seeing an image of the subject on his television monitor in the corner the subject was visiting while out-of-body. The experimenter was unaware of which corner the subject was supposed to go to, and he did not know which was a control period and which an OOBE period.

I mention these studies just to point out that there has already been some work done in the field that is difficult to explain away, although many people continue to do so. The scientific community as a whole is incredibly resistant to the concept of nonphysical existence. Extrasensory perception is OK, but out-of-body experiences seem to really challenge the way many people think.

Another phenomenon that lends support to the validity of nonphysical experience is mutual dreams or mutual OOBEs. Here two or more people meet in a dream or OOBE; upon their return to physical reality, they both remember the same conversations and experiences. An example of such an experience is included in Fox's book.[4] Fox and two friends, Slade and Elkington, decided to meet at Southhampton Common that night in their dreams. Fox dreamt that he met Elkington at the specified location, and they both realized they were dreaming. They commented on the conspicuous absence of their third friend. The next day, Fox asked Elkington whether he had dreamed the previous night. Elkington replied that he had met Fox at the specified location and realized that he was dreaming, "but old Slade didn't turn up. We had just time to greet each other and comment on his absence, then the dream ended." Slade later told Fox that he had not dreamt at all that night. To those who bring up the issue that the dreamers were expecting to meet in advance, Fox points out that *all three* were expecting to meet.

An example of a mutual OOBE can be found in Richard Bach's autobiographical book *The Bridge Across Forever*.[5] After about six months practice, Bach and his wife, Leslie, accomplished their first mutual out-of-body.

Bach found himself sitting in the air over his bed and saw "a radiant form afloat" right next to him. It was Leslie, and they were able to communicate without words. She told him she was already out and had "coaxed" him out. Together they floated up through the ceiling and proceeded to share a memorable experience. They were abruptly awakened by one of their cats and a few moments later simultaneously remembered their journey. According to Bach, "After the first year's practice, we could meet together out of body several times a month; the suspicion that we were visitors on the planet grew till we could smile at each other, interested observers, in the middle of the evening news."

The phenomenon of mutual dreams and OOBEs certainly lends a modicum of support to the concept of objective nonphysical experience. Since it is not something that can easily be done in a laboratory, it is often swept under the rug or minimized as being just a form of telepathy or clairvoyance.

In this book, we will study the art of leaving the body from a subjective rather than scientific perspective. With all due respect, the framework of scientific research and investigation is simply too limiting for would-be astral explorers. The domain of science deals with effects that are observable and measurable through the physical senses. When scientists investigate phenomena like OOBEs, they are ultimately limited to dealing with nonphysical experiences from a physical perspective. They can only record descriptions of those who do it, measure effects that can be produced in physical reality, try to physically detect the nonphysical "body," and so on.

To truly investigate OOBEs, one must be willing to bend or even abandon the rules of scientific inquiry. Much of what we human beings can learn through exploring inner reality cannot even be put into words, let alone proven scientifically. *The true exploration of this ancient art form is in the doing.* We can get answers. We can have peak experiences of knowing and wisdom that will enrich our lives and our beings. But in order to do this, we may have to leave some of the old frameworks behind.

The greatest value in the study of OOBEs has little to do with electroencephalograms, rapid eye movements, or even the ability to describe a mountain thousands of miles away. The greatest value is in the exhilaration of being out-of-body oneself, the intuitive comprehensions received, and the glimpses of the mysteries of the universe that are available to the bold explorer.

2
BENEFITS OF ASTRAL PROJECTION

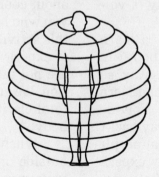

Some of you may never have had an OOBE. Whether you realize it or not, though, we have all been out of our bodies on numerous occasions during sleep. Surveys conducted by Hart, Green, Haraldsson, and others, indicate that the OOBE is not a rare occurrence.[1] From my own experience with people interested in metaphysics, however, it seems that relatively few have developed the ability to voluntarily induce these experiences.

But why would anyone want to learn how to consciously leave his or her body? In the end we all have to leave them anyway, so what's the hurry? And even if we can learn how to travel outside of our bodies, how do we know we'll be able to find our way back?

On the other hand, if it's true that people can learn how to induce out-of-body experiences, we may have access to a whole new and vast area of human potential—one that may shed light on some of the fundamental questions humankind has always asked. Is death the end or just another beginning? If we do survive death, to what degree will we still know ourselves as ourselves? What's the greater purpose behind our lives on this fascinating and sometimes tumultuous planet? What's really going on here?

Explorations outside of your body can tremendously expand your understanding about your life and your universe. For those of you who have had little or no experience with this activity, it is important to note what kind of experience we are really talking about. We are *not* talking about some vague hallucination. We *are* talking about achieving a state of total clarity and aliveness while out of your body.

When you find yourself fully conscious outside of your body and it feels *as real* as your normal physical experience, you begin to stop and wonder. When you have had this experience several times, it becomes difficult to dismiss it as a fluke or figment of your imagination, and it might well begin to alter the way you look at your universe. These experiences are often so extraordinary and powerful that they can affect some of your most fundamental belief systems.

LEARNING TO LIVE WITH ETERNAL LIFE

People who have had a vivid OOBE often regard it as one of the most intense experiences of their lives. The OOBE provides them with a natural and exciting opportunity to experience identity independent of physical form while they are still alive. Their belief systems about death are often radically changed. They have actually experienced the sensation of being unmistakably alive and conscious while seemingly detached from their physical bodies. Although their experi-

ences do not constitute scientific proof, they often feel that they now simply *know* their existence is not dependent on their physical bodies. For individuals who fear death, these experiences often result in a significant reduction of that fear. Those who already believe in life after death may find that their explorations outside of the body enable them to comprehend this on a much deeper, emotional level.

A new belief system about death can have a truly powerful effect on how you live your life. For me, it was only after I had OOBEs that I really began to understand that this physical reality is just one stop along the path of our greater existence. Many people go through life fearing their death or thinking death does not now concern them and therefore miss out on the great wisdom and perspective they can gain from using death as a teacher.

As a result of the out-of-body experiences I have had over the years, I can now honestly say that I have little, if any, fear of death. On the contrary, I am really looking forward to it, and I fully expect it to be exciting and fun. This does not mean that I am in a hurry to leave this reality, because I'm not. I just know, on an intuitive level, that when my time to leave this reality comes, I will find myself outside of my physical body, fully alive, fully conscious, still knowing myself as myself and ready to party.

It was only when I understood that the ballgame is going to go into extra innings that I was able to look death in the face, so to speak, and really listen to its teaching. Since I am no longer afraid of or uncomfortable about death, I am more inclined to focus on the reality of life's temporariness and use it for inspiration. This focus makes me want to maximize my life in every way. It helps me understand that the moments I spend with the people I love are completely unique, and even

if I will know them in other times or other universes, things will never again be quite the same. It helps me cut through all the nonsense and pettiness that is so easy to think is important. It helps me savor and use my energy instead of squandering it. It helps me give up worry and enjoy my day.

I often deliberately remind myself how truly temporary our physical lives are. Although I also believe that each moment is eternal, the moments of our days represent the point of our aliveness; each is unique and precious. If we waste these moments, if we procrastinate, if we do not pursue what we love and try to do the things we want to do, we have only ourselves to blame.

The ongoing awareness that death is not the end can affect your whole mode of operation. When you really understand that you are going to live forever, you may find you are inclined to adjust some of your goals and aspirations. If the ballgame is really going to continue indefinitely, understanding the greater purpose of your participation in it becomes an even more important issue.

Again, we are not talking here just about intellectual understanding but about a deep, emotional comprehension that your identity will survive death. The out-of-body experience can transmit this emotional comprehension in a way that is hard to match with any physical experience alone.

PRACTICING FOR TRANSITION DAY

A surprisingly large number of people who have been close to death or were clinically dead and then revived have reported near-death experiences (NDE) that were relatively consistent. One of the elements of the classic NDE is an out-of-body experience. In one study, 37 percent of a sample of people who had come close to death had experienced something akin to an OOBE before they were revived.[2] It is not unusual for people who have had NDEs to report finding themselves in their hospital rooms looking down at their physical bodies before going on to the next stage of the NDE.

We may as well familiarize ourselves with the out-of-body state because that is what we are going to be dealing with immediately after death. I believe that those who are familiar and adept with OOBEs will find the whole death experience less disorienting. After all, you don't die every day, and a little preparation will make for a smoother and more enjoyable trip.

PATHWAY TO KNOWLEDGE

More and more people are becoming disenchanted with the fundamental belief systems underlying our civilization. Many are no longer satisfied with the old myths, rules, and regulations of conventional religions or the limited framework of understanding offered by science. People have begun to look elsewhere for answers. Sooner or later, students of metaphysics turn their attention to the possibility of dimensions of existence that are outside the domain of our normal physical senses. The OOBE is an enticing and obvious option for anyone attempting a thorough and open-minded exploration of what really makes the universe tick.

Certainly one of the most valuable benefits of practicing OOBEs is that it can provide access to direct-knowing experiences and to the inner realms of existence to which we will all eventually return. Along with a new awareness of life and death, the OOBE can provide you with an experiential sense of what physical reality truly is, for when you literally pop back and forth between worlds, you begin to feel and know that your normal waking reality is not nearly as solid as you once thought.

Of course, physicists already know that matter is not solid. They have stated and restated that everything around us—chairs, buildings, even our bodies—are composed of space and atoms. The atoms, we are told, are really a whirlwind of subatomic particles moving at speeds we can barely imagine. Matter, we are told, is fundamentally equivalent to energy. Thus, we are all energy beings, living in an amazing energy universe.

OOBEs can also help you increase your intuitive understanding about what's really going on here. You will be able to sense, in a way that ultimately cannot be put into words, that the physical world is really just one channel on the multidimensional cosmic television set. We are tuned into a specific band of frequencies, and most of the time that is all we perceive. Learning to leave the body is like discovering, for the first time, that you can change the channels on your television set.

There is a tremendous difference between theorizing about other worlds and actually traveling to them. When you achieve interdimensional travel, including the sensations that accompany it, your new experiences of how the universe really is can become a part of you. It goes beyond intellectual comprehension. The experience itself can change you. It can enrich the colors of your days. The knowledge you can gain is like an overlay through which you sometimes look and see the world in a shimmering, more expansive, and translucent light.

In short, OOBE work is an obvious choice for anyone interested in exploring the complex and mysterious energy universe we all inhabit. With practice, you can use it effectively as a doorway to intuitional knowledge and direct-knowing experiences.

Once you have the basics down, you can literally have a field day while out-of-body. The educational opportunities abound. You can, for example, simply ask to meet a guide or a teacher. Or you can decide to meet a reincarnational self face-to-face. Perhaps you would like to travel to a distant star or walk through your bedroom wall. Or maybe you've been wondering about the possibility of time travel and would like to explore the centuries firsthand. I hope I don't sound too much like a travel agent when I say that all this and more can be yours if you sign up for this adventure. And signing up simply means committing some time and energy to learning the art of astral travel.

FUN AND GAMES

I have said that practicing OOBEs is educational, inspirational, and practical. I would now like to add that perhaps the most obvious reason for practicing OOBEs is that it's incredibly fun. I am talking here about playtime with a capital *P*. I have had some of the most exciting and ecstatic experiences of my life while out-of-body.

Our unlimited energy and the natural joy of our existence are ever present if we allow ourselves to feel it. Somehow the kind of experiences you can have while out of your body can help reawaken an awareness of the magic of the universe, both physical and nonphysical. Although sometimes we forget just how amazing it is that we exist in bodies that know how to walk, breathe, grow, and heal themselves, there are things we can do to help us get back in touch with our inner knowing. Play can help us do that, for when we play we have greater access to this inner knowledge.

There are many different "games" to play to get in touch with the joy and wisdom that are our birthright. One is the game of leaving the physical body with full awareness. In order to become proficient at this game, it is important to practice with a playful attitude. In this manner, you undoubtedly will learn at an accelerated rate and enjoy yourself all along the way.

3
ESSENTIAL METAPHYSICS

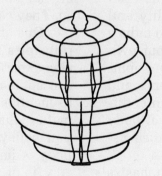

If you spur your imagination with belief, desire and expectancy, and train it to visualize your goals so that you see, feel, hear, taste, and touch them, you will get what you want.[1]

José Silva

Webster's dictionary defines *metaphysics* as "a division of philosophy that is concerned with the fundamental nature of reality and being. . . ." If you want to learn how to induce OOBEs, the place to start is with your own metaphysical assumptions, that is, your opinions and attitudes about your existence and your universe. Individuals who encounter difficulty in their attempts to get out-of-body generally need to examine and alter their belief systems.

It is extremely important to reemphasize here that the experiences an individual encounters while out-of-body will be greatly determined by his or her attitudes. An individual with extremely limiting beliefs will probably be unable to take advantage of the benefits mentioned in the last chapter even if he or she does learn how to have OOBEs. In addition, belief systems might very well be the most significant factor in whether or not an individual is successful in learning how to induce OOBEs to begin with. Belief systems are not static, however, unless we make them so. They can be changed.

One of the most important metaphysical principles I have learned is that thought creates experience. We will shortly explore this concept in more depth, but for now I just want to mention that this principle holds true no matter what dimension you find yourself in. If you believe that existence outside of your body is improbable or that intuitive knowledge is of little value, your beliefs may prevent you from taking advantage of the OOBE benefits. If you strongly believe that an OOBE must be some form of hallucination or that the existence of other valid dimensions is a child's fairy tale not to be taken seriously, you may inhibit intuitional knowledge that would otherwise be available to you. In fact, your beliefs will color both your experience and your access to knowledge whether you are in or out of your body.

A basic understanding of metaphysics can make it far easier to induce OOBEs and help inner explorers get the most out of their nonphysical journeys. If you are planning to travel to other dimensions of experience—or even if you just want to fly around your own neighborhood—it will be helpful to have some basic concepts under your belt.

••••••●••••••

THE PHYSICAL UNIVERSE IS JUST ONE OF THE INFINITE DIMENSIONS THAT EXIST.

••••••●••••••

When our consciousness is set to a certain energy frequency, we are here. When we learn how to change frequencies with our consciousness, we will find ourselves in other worlds.

Our eyes can see only a limited range of light. Our ears can hear only a certain range of sound. In essence, we can perceive only a very small band of the possible energy frequencies out there. It is not only shortsighted but incredibly egotistical to conclude that the energy waves, or frequencies, we perceive as our world are the only world. Learning how to leave the body and bring the waking consciousness along for the ride is a simple and obvious way to get firsthand evidence of these other valid realms of existence.

••••••●••••••

THE PHYSICAL WORLD IS AN ELEMENTARY SCHOOL FOR COSMIC CITIZENS.

••••••●••••••

We are all enrolled in a cosmic grade school, and we are here to learn. In the fertile soil of physical reality we are meant to grow and blossom. And to the degree that we are able to take advantage of it, we are invited to enjoy the fruits of our own creativity and love.

Our day-to-day experience is our classroom, and we are learning the ABCs of using universal energy. We are being trained to become responsible citizens of the universe. We are all infant gods of sorts, learning how to take our first steps toward becoming artful creators in cooperation with the Universal Mind (or God, or All That Is, or whatever term you prefer). In this regard, we each already have access to practically unlimited energy.

••••••••••

EVERY SINGLE EVENT IN YOUR LIFE HAS BEEN DRAWN INTO YOUR EXPERIENCE ACCORDING TO THE IDEAS AND THOUGHTS THAT YOU HOLD IN YOUR MIND.

••••••••••

This is perhaps the most important fundamental concept to understand. Napoleon Hill corroborates this idea in his famous book *Think and Grow Rich*, in which he says, "All thoughts which have been emotionalized (given feeling) and mixed with faith, begin immediately to translate themselves into their physical equivalent or counterpart."[2]

What we focus on in our minds becomes manifest in our experience. Our current life situation, with all of its nuances, is a result of the thoughts and ideas on which we focus.

We are each learning how to get a handle on the awesome power of our own minds. A frequent focus on fearful thoughts and ideas will draw like experience into your life. For example, many people believe that we live in a dog-eat-dog world. An individual who focuses strongly on such a belief will find that the people and events in his or her personal life confirm it. Likewise, if instead an individual chooses to believe that humankind is inherently good and focuses on its best attributes, his or her experience will confirm this viewpoint. The art form we are learning is how to evaluate, select, and alter the ingredients of our own minds and thus consciously create our own experience.

Nothing accidental ever happens. All events are created through imagination and belief. If someone drops a penny from a skyscraper and it just "happens" to land on your head, it's no accident. If your life is filled with love, enjoyable work, nature, health, and abundance, it's no accident. If you become a successful astral explorer, it's no accident. If you have ever been robbed or otherwise "victimized," it is your own fears, feelings of worthlessness, or negative imaginings that have brought these unpleasant experiences into your life.

One of the issues that arises for many people when they work with this idea is the "burden" of taking responsibility for everything in their lives. When people realize the power of their own thoughts, they sometimes get nervous about it. They may get worried about every little negative thought or imagining that pops into their heads.

First of all, a few (so-called) negative thoughts or fears are not so powerful that they will outweigh the thrust of a basically positive mental climate. Thoughts and emotions have a natural flow. Different types of thoughts and emotions will move and change as long as you do not block them. It's only when you *focus* on "negative" thoughts and beliefs that you create difficulties.

Second, it's far more of a burden to be powerless over the events in your life than to be responsible for them. Creating your own experience doesn't mean you should examine your failures or weaknesses and then feel guilty. It means that you have power—power to create changes and make things more to your liking. This is hardly a burden.

The true understanding and incorporation of this concept into an individual's life represents a milestone in his or her overall spiritual growth. It is one of the most crucial lessons that we are to learn during our tenure in the classroom called physical reality. To understand it fully can transform your life.

This fundamental truth—that thought is the architect of experience—has always been available to humankind. At the time of this writing, it has been steadily gaining recognition in New Age circles and showing up frequently in recent metaphysical literature. I hope this trend continues, for if enough people begin to understand the nature of their power to mold their world, we shall see a healing on a planetary scale.

When I was younger, I used to wonder why there was so much disagreement in the world about everything. How did we wind up with so many different interpretations of reality? Why do people *believe* their beliefs so strongly? Why is everyone so stubborn about his or her point of view? Only later did I realize that people are stubborn about their viewpoints because their experience always gives them evidence to back up whatever they believe. Until people make the connection between their ideas and the events in their lives, they will be missing a crucial point. Just because they have physical evidence to support their ideas does not mean that their way of looking at things is the way things really are or are meant to be.

As our understanding increases, we learn to recognize belief systems that are more conducive to creative living and joy and are truer to the nature of our beings. We learn to move toward these expensive frameworks by being flexible and by experimenting with what works best for us. We are meant to freely play with our ideas, try them, watch them materialize, reevaluate, make changes, and generally focus on a point of view that brings us a fulfilling life. Any area of your life in which you don't like what's going on, you can just as easily create your heart's desire.

But what about birth conditions, you might wonder. People obviously are born into widely differing situations. I believe that we all choose our parents and our birth conditions too in accordance with our own goals and those of our "higher" selves. There are tremendous differences here with respect to how various identities like to learn and, according to their level of development, how wisely they make their choices. As we each grow from infancy to adulthood, however, we can use our power to change our life situations.

My real introduction to this life-transforming concept came when I was attending Jane Roberts's classes in the early 70s. Seth, the nonphysical teacher channeled through Jane, constantly spoke of the importance of understanding that we each create our own reality with our thoughts, emotions, and beliefs. It is highly important that this not be only an intellectual understanding. Seth taught that when you affirm your own being, trust your spontaneous direction, and understand that you create your own reality on an emotional, intellectual, and intuitive level, your consciousness will tune into a "higher" state of functioning in which intuition and intellect merge. Comprehensions will flow into your consciousness and become part of you. You will notice that things seem to be going your way more than ever before. Jane Roberts's book *The Nature of Personal Reality: A Seth Book* delves into all of these issues and is a truly excellent treatise on creating your own reality.[3]

As I began to work with these concepts, I found there was something inside of me that strongly resonated with them. I did not, however, fully believe them on an emotional level. I wasn't about to give up my doubts so easily. I wanted some proof. And the only way to prove to yourself that you have what amounts to magic power is to actually use that power and see it work for yourself.

I began looking at those areas of my life in which I was unhappy about what was going on. If I really created my own reality, that meant I could make changes in those areas. I began to observe myself to see if I could find the thoughts and emotions that were associated with the trouble spots in my life. Most of them were easy to find since I was obviously feeding myself certain negative suggestions frequently. Others were a bit tougher to find because they were thoughts and emotions that I had but didn't "approve of" anymore, so they were less apparent. They seemed to become apparent, however, as I continued a determined, honest examination of my conscious mind.

I traced the thoughts and emotions to the beliefs that were producing them; I then proceeded to change the beliefs. Changing a belief is not fundamentally difficult—but of course, if you believe it is difficult, that is how it will be. It is really a matter of controlling your focus of attention. By using simple self-hypnosis techniques, you *can* change your beliefs fairly easily as long as you are *willing* to do so.

To make a long story short, in every area that I applied these principles my "magic" power worked. It didn't happen all at once. It took awhile before I really began to understand, on an emotional level, that I had this power. Gradually, though, as I changed beliefs and saw the results materialize time and time again, the belief in my own power became my new *modus operandi*.

This magic, by the way, is really quite scientific. It simply represents a level of scientific understanding far beyond our current one. We don't have to understand the intricacies of how our bodies move in order to move our feet. The same applies to using our power. Our ability to create whatever we wish in our lives is as natural to us as our heartbeats.

The personal world we each live in, with all of its unique characters, friends, loved ones, dramas, challenges, joys, and sorrows, is a direct reflection of our inner mental and emotional states of mind. If you want to alter the outer scenario, you must learn how to alter the inner one.

No one can prove to you that your beliefs, thoughts, emotions, and imaginings are always reflected in your world. I know that this is true from my own experience and inner knowledge. Each individual must learn this crucial bit of information for themselves by actually using their own awesome power to manipulate their personal worlds. When people see for themselves the direct connection between what they focus on in their minds and the events that enter their lives, they will start to understand that we are all indeed miraculous beings, with potentials and abilities that we are only beginning to discover.

Once you learn the simple technology of accessing your power, you can apply this to your work with OOBEs. OOBEs provide an excellent opportunity to practice the art of manipulating your experience. In other words, if you really want to leave your body with full awareness, you've got what it takes to make it happen. Anyone can have OOBEs if he or she is willing to examine and, if necessary, alter those beliefs that impact on this ability.

You are responsible for your experience no matter what dimension you are in. Your thoughts create your reality in the out-of-body state, too. In fact, one of the things that crops up fairly frequently in the OOBE literature is the responsiveness to thoughts of the out-of-body state.

When I am out of my body it appears that my thoughts create events at a far faster rate than normal. It seems that in some nonphysical realities thoughts are more or less instantly materialized. The physical world seems to operate at a slower rate of materialization, and I believe that there is a very important reason for this. We are at the beginning stages of understanding our power. The elementary school known as physical reality has, in certain terms and to some degree, been childproofed; it has been deliberately set up in such a way that it takes time before a thought becomes materialized. Those thoughts that are materialized in physical reality are thoughts that have reached a certain level of concentration and intensity. Obviously, not every stray thought or fear is literally materialized, or we would all be in serious trouble!

I believe we are being prepared to graduate to dimensions of existence in which thoughts and emotions are materialized both instantly and with a finesse that will astound us. We won't be ready for these worlds until we become adept in our use of energy. We *will* learn, however, and we will fulfill the awesome potential that is our natural heritage.

4
THE ABCs OF USING POWER

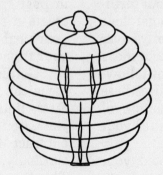

Imagination . . . is one of the motivating agencies that helps transform your beliefs into physical experience.[1]

Seth

All of the exciting possibilities discussed in the previous chapter are just a bunch of words until you have had your own actual experiences with the power that is your birthright. It is not difficult, however, to get your own evidence. This chapter will briefly cover the fundamentals of working with your ideas and gaining access to your power. The following chapters show you how to utilize these principles to succeed in the induction of OOBEs and how to get the most out of your nonphysical excursions.

As the previous chapter suggested, your ideas are not just inert substances stored in your physical brain. They are structures composed of a form of energy as real as electricity or microwaves. These structures produce thoughts, emotions, and imaginings. Your imagination resonates with your ideas. Your future experience will be the outcome of what you imagine, think, and feel in the present moment. Your current experience is the outcome of what you imagined, thought, and felt in past "present" moments. If you want to create a future significantly different from your current experience, you must restructure your framework of ideas.

Getting a handle on your framework of ideas can be divided into three basic steps. First, find out what your ideas really are. Next, decide which ideas you want to add or subtract. Finally, reprogram your mind accordingly, and change your mental climate. This is an ongoing process.

INTROSPECTION

The refreshing news about this whole procedure is that your ideas are readily accessible as long as you are willing to be honest with yourself.

Probably one of the simplest ways to examine your beliefs is to monitor your thoughts at various points of the day. Your ideas are, more or less, directly expressed by your thoughts. At different times of the day, observe the various trains of thought on which you seem to focus. What beliefs do these thoughts represent?

Another easy technique is to simply write down your ideas on the specific area you are examining. For example, if you are examining your ideas about relationships, you can simply write a mini-essay on the subject to try to discover whether you are holding any ideas that are no longer serving you.

You may wish to begin working in those areas in which you are clearly dissatisfied. Or you may wish to explore all the important areas of your life so that you can then stimulate all-around growth.

Your dreams can also be a great source of information and insight about your mental climate. Working with your dreams on a regular basis can be tremendously valuable for examining as well as altering belief systems. We will discuss this further in Chapter 8.

If you are so inclined, you may want to use your emotions to discover beliefs. Often our limited concepts of how we "should" behave and what we "should" feel result in a selective repression of certain emotions. Some emotions we think are inappropriate, some we disapprove of, and some we simply fear.

To say that the repression of emotion has caused humankind considerable difficulty is an understatement.

Allowing yourself to feel the full range of your emotions means acknowledging and feeling whatever you are feeling and letting your emotions flow naturally. To use emotions to discover beliefs, simply let yourself fully feel an emotion and then track it to the thoughts and beliefs that come up in association with it. Changing the beliefs will change the emotions.

Discovering your beliefs requires work, but it is not inherently difficult. There is no issue, challenge, or problem in your current life that you cannot deal with. No matter what your past, your current situation is a result of your "contemporary" climate of belief.

SELECTING NEW IDEAS

We have all been greatly affected by our parents and teachers and the belief systems that surrounded us as we were growing up. If we heard a belief again and again from significant people in our lives, we probably accepted that belief. That belief then became manifest in our personal world and thus became more firmly entrenched. Many such beliefs may have been accepted without the benefit of our best critical judgment.

The "usual" way of operating cannot be part of this selection of new beliefs. It makes no sense to base your selection solely on your experience because your experience is a result of your beliefs. New criteria are needed. Everyone must find his or her own path with this stuff, but I'll share with you some of the guidelines I have used: Select ideas that breathe life and beauty into your experience;

reject ideas that downgrade your worth or power. Select ideas that bring you what you want; reject ideas that limit your joy or impede the free flow of your energy. Listen to your intuitions. Trust them. Let them be your guide, along with your intellect, when making your belief selections.

For example, if you believe it's hard to make a buck in this world, you may wish to change this belief to something less limiting. Try believing that you can easily and creatively attract abundance in all areas of your life. If you believe that old age is a valueless, torturous stage to go through, it would be advisable to change this point of view. Your experience will *always* reflect what you have been focusing on. It is better to work things out in your mind than to continue running into the effects of inferior beliefs in your daily life.

Again, this is an ongoing process. Beliefs on which you choose to focus now may not serve your purposes at some future point; then you can select new ones.

ALTERATIONS

There are different ways to approach the issue of changing your ideas, imaginings, thoughts, and emotions, but most are actually a type of self-hypnosis.

All day long we act as our own hypnotists by constantly feeding ourselves mental suggestions. We tell ourselves that we are fit or fat, rich or poor, healthy or sick, or something in between. When people undergo a radical change of belief, like becoming members of a cult, they usually have utilized hypnosis, allowing themselves to be hypnotized into accepting a specific dogma and continuing to hypnotize themselves into believing it. On a more positive note, when people suddenly seem to have dramatically improved their self-images, they also have utilized self-hypnosis by changing the focus of their inner dialogues to more positive suggestions about themselves.

•••••●●•••••

WE HAVE THE POWER TO HYPNOTIZE OURSELVES INTO BELIEVING WHATEVER IT IS THAT WE WANT TO BELIEVE.

•••••●●•••••

Scary as it might sound, we do have this ability. In fact, we are continually hypnotizing ourselves to believe what we currently believe. So, you see, changing beliefs is not fundamentally difficult. It seems difficult sometimes because people are reluctant to relinquish their hold on old beliefs and take a chance on hypnotizing themselves into believing new ones. Allowing yourself to deliberately believe something for which you may not yet have physical evidence runs contrary to standard operating procedure. The evidence will follow, but only *after* you have altered your belief

ACTING ON YOUR NEW BELIEFS

When you reprogram your mind, new opportunities and urges will appear in your life. In order to take advantage of these opportunities, you must begin to base your actions on your new ways of thinking. You must act on the new urges in order to materialize them.

Here's an example of what I mean. Let's say you are single and looking to create a love relationship. You have worked on your beliefs about being worthy of love and about creating a meeting with the right person. Through the power of your thoughts, that special someone shows up at the laundromat. You don't know this yet, but this person has already known you through countless lifetimes. You feel a strong urge to meet this person. At this point you can (a) smile and try to strike up a conversation, (b) ask to borrow some detergent, or (c) run for your life. If you choose (c), you obviously will not get what you want. Backing up your beliefs with action is a crucial part of the process of materialization.

We will shortly work on beliefs relevant to your upcoming work with OOBEs. Once you have made any needed adjustments in your belief systems, you will have to act on the adjusted beliefs in order to materialize your goal of inducing OOBEs. In other words, you must back up your OOBE goals with consistent practice, just as you would when learning any other skill.

RESISTANCE TO CHANGE

Another issue that comes up for some people is a fear of change in general. Change is something we all have to deal with anyway, but actively manipulating your reality means accelerating change. It is important, therfore, to trust in your spontaneous direction, including the changes that occur as you move freely through the pathways of your existence. Your natural energy and intuition will indicate where you and your inner wisdom want you to go. Really trusting yourself and letting yourself go is a shortcut to spiritual growth and to ridding yourself of limiting beliefs. In this book we are using a holistic approach to learning the art of inducing OOBEs. Although most of the exercises are specifically geared to OOBEs, some general belief alteration practice will help you prepare for the OOBE belief work. The ability to consciously manipulate the contents of your mind is an invaluable skill that can be used to achieve success with OOBEs or any other area. The following is a general exercise for working with beliefs.

Exercise 1: General Belief Work

You will need a pen and a notebook.

Procedure: Select some areas from the following list (or any other specific area that you want to work on). For each area, follow the six steps. Work on one area at a time.

Yourself	Your children
Work	Health
Relationships	Your intuition
Sex	Your spouse
Your body	Your power
Your worth	Men
Aging	Women
	Money

1. Write a few paragraphs (or pages) describing the full range of your thoughts, feelings, and beliefs in the area you have selected.
2. Examine what you have written. Try to crystallize your beliefs into one or two simple, concise statements.
3. Using your intuitions and intellect, decide which beliefs are limiting or no longer serving you.
4. For any beliefs that you think are limiting you, formulate and write out a new belief that is more expansive and positive. It may very well be the opposite of your previous limiting belief.
5. Crystallize your new beliefs into simple, concise statements or affirmations. Utilize the present tense as if the new belief were already true. Here are some examples:

• My body is aerobically fit, muscularly strong, and brimming with health and energy.

• I am an important part of the universe. I respect myself and treat myself well.

- I spend my time doing things I love to do. This lifestyle automatically attracts abundance in every area of my life.

6. Devote a few minutes a day to reprogramming yourself through self-hypnosis.

Simply quiet your mind and repeat your affirmation statements to yourself. Say them with feeling. For those few minutes, allow yourself to believe that they are true. Imagine that you have already achieved whatever it is that you want.

5
GETTING RID OF FEAR

In general, the only thing standing between an individual and learning how to induce OOBEs is his or her own attitudes. Some people, for example, may think that the practice of leaving the body is tampering with forces we weren't meant to touch. After all, according to more conventional modes of thinking, OOBE practitioners appear to be leaving their bodies ahead of the official schedule.

Many, if not most, of us were raised in an environment of beliefs that did not include the validity of such "strange" experiences. Indeed, such activities might be considered downright unwholesome by conventional or fundamentalist religions. Despite both religious and scientific prejudice, however, people persist in reporting these ethereal excursions, and parapsychologists continue to verify that humankind possesses paranormal abilities.

Many who have experienced a brief and involuntary OOBE would like to go for another ride, only this time with a little more control. Then there are those who have not yet experienced an OOBE but yearn to try because of curiosity, a drive to understand their universe, or simply love of adventure.

Those who wish to learn this art form may find that they have some religious or scientific prejudices of their own to deal with. They may find that certain fears surface when they start practicing their new craft in earnest. If not addressed, these fears can impede their progress or completely short-circuit their efforts.

Some would-be astral adventurers may find it hard to believe that they can experience total clarity and consciousness outside of the physical body. Or perhaps they think others can do it but are not sufficiently in touch with their own personal power to understand that they can do it, too.

Therefore, before we start focusing on techniques, we will learn how to create an environment of mental energy that is ripe for the deliberate induction of out-of-body experiences. I cannot emphasize enough how crucial the mental environment is regarding the ability to induce OOBEs and the quality of the experiences generated. Which technique you decide to use for leaving the body may not be the most important factor. The key factor for many people is the intensity of their desire, their mental climate, and their ability to use their power to create what they want in their lives.

Furthermore, you will probably be unable to effectively utilize OOBE induction techniques if your mental atmosphere is either too limiting or clouded by fear. If your current attitudes are not conducive to the induction of OOBEs, we will attempt to change them so that they will be.

Before you begin the belief work in the next chapter, we will examine what is probably the biggest obstacle for many people. That obstacle is fear. Feeling unsafe about inducing

OOBEs can interfere with your attempts to experience them. And even if you do succeed in getting out, fear can still get in the way. Sometimes people aren't even aware of their fears until they are actually out of their bodies or starting to go out.

A case in point is an OOBE described by a student of mine, John, who has had about a half dozen involuntary OOBEs, most of which occurred while he was sleeping or about to go to sleep:

In the half dozen times that I spontaneously found myself out of my physical body, usually within a minute or so I started feeling intense fears for no apparent reason. When I'm awake, I don't have any fear about it. When I'm actually experiencing it, something gets to me. I can remember very vividly one time as I was waking up in the morning, about an hour before I would normally get out of bed, I started rising straight up out of bed. I knew that I was out-of-body. So far I was calm and doing pretty good. I just kept floating until I got to the ceiling. I started to go through the ceiling, into the room that was upstairs. Then I got stuck in the ceiling. I didn't know that could happen. I said to myself "OK, I'm out of my body. This is my astral form. Fine. I'm in the ceiling. I can't go up. I can't go down. I'm going to be here forever." I got frightened and started to panic and feel disoriented, and I immediately snapped back to my physical body and jumped out of my physical bed. . . . Other times that I found myself out of my body, I'd start out curious and actually excited and happy that I was out again and would have the opportunity to experiment with the state. That didn't last long, though, because I would get fearful again. That would always end the experience immediately, and I would wind up back in my physical body. I'm usually angry and frustrated when the experience is over, because I

wanted it to continue for a longer period of time. . . . What's frustrating to me is that I don't know what I'm afraid of. It's just a feeling of fear. . . . It seems pretty common because I have friends who have had similar experiences. We want to have the experiences and then it happens spontaneously, but there always seems to be this fear of the unknown.

It appears that in the above experience, John became afraid of something specific, that is, getting stuck in the ceiling. Yet John became afraid every time he found himself out; the other times had nothing to do with getting stuck. I questioned John about what he was afraid of, and he rejected all the possibilities I came up with. John stated firmly that he really didn't know what he was afraid of. "Fear of the unknown" was the only way he could describe it. John's experience of being stuck in the ceiling was probably a result of his underlying fears—something to which his deeper fear attached itself, so to speak. A general remedy you can use in such situations, is to remind yourself that you are creating the situation with your own thoughts, and tell yourself that you are free to move. Giving yourself such suggestions while out-of-body often produces surprisingly immediate results.

Some people are afraid of more specific things than John was—being unable to find the way back, running into someone or something unfriendly, or accidentally severing the alleged "silver cord." All of these fears are basically groundless, but nevertheless they can interfere with the induction of OOBEs. And even if you do succeed in getting out, whether deliberately or spontaneously, these kinds of fears can either cut the experience short or simply ruin the fun. So if you have any fear-oriented beliefs that you think might get in your way, it will be particularly important for you to make adjustments when you begin your belief work for OOBEs in the next chapter. And note that despite the fear John felt whenever he had a spontaneous OOBE, he always found himself back in his physical body, safe and sound.

FINDING THE WAY BACK

Some people are afraid that if they leave their bodies they might die. In the same vein is the fear of getting lost and being unable to find one's way back.

I have never had any problems returning to my physical body. Many others who have had numerous OOBEs, including people such as Oliver Fox, Sylvan Muldoon, and Robert Monroe, who have written books on the subject, have obviously managed to find their way back to their bodies also—or else they could not have written their books.

Of course, it could be argued that if someone decided to leave his or her body permanently, he or she would not be around to tell the story. I can tell you only that we have all already left our bodies numerous times in the sleep state; we are just learning how to become more proficient and conscious about it.

It is possible to experience a temporary, self-created difficulty in returning to the body, but this generally is due to the practitioner's lack of understanding of how responsive the experience is to his or her own thoughts. If you ever find yourself in such a situation, simply relax and realize that it is your own thinking that is causing the difficulty. Tell yourself that you can return to your body anytime you want, and simply visualize your body and will yourself back. You will shortly find yourself back in your physical body anyway.

A student named Roseanne, who attended my course on out-of-bodies and dreams and apparently needed to address and resolve certain fears before she would allow herself to induce OOBEs, describes her situation.

Many times before I came to this class I started to have an out-of-body experience, but I always caught myself and awakened with this jolt of terror. I think that I had a very strong fear of dying. What usually happened is that this tremendous shock of fear would come and I would bolt upright to a sitting position. When you talked in class about the similarity between the after-death state and out-of-bodies, and that the only time we die is when we choose to die, and that it was perfectly safe to do out-of-bodies, that really helped me.

Following is Roseanne's account of her first successful OOBE. The induction technique she used is described in Chapter 10 as Technique #1. Just prior to the experience, Roseanne suggested to herself that it was safe to go out-of-body and that when she actually started to leave her body, she would remind herself that it was safe.

My body was asleep, but I was conscious and felt myself starting to move straight up and out of my body. The same fear started, and I wanted to wake up quick, but then I remembered the suggestion. I told myself, "No, it's OK. I'm safe!" And there was just this little extra push, this kind of change, and then I went out of my body. I hung around in my room that first time. I kept going back into my body every few minutes just to check out that it was still there. I kept going in and out, in and out. And that was the first time.

It appears that two things allowed Roseanne to have an OOBE where before she would have blocked the experience. First, Roseanne seemed to reduce her fear that she might die if she had an OOBE. In essence, she shifted her belief system in this area. Assuming that individuals create their own reality, it follows that they will not die until they are good and ready. Therefore, consciously leaving your body for fun and edification poses no more threat than walking to the grocery store. Roseanne reported that her feelings shifted to believing that "death is not something that happens to us—we choose what is going to happen."

Second, as part of her induction method, Roseanne used suggestions that addressed her specific concerns. She gave herself these suggestions at two crucial points: just prior to the OOBE attempt and again at the exact moment she began to lift out of her body. Suggestions you give yourself once you are out of your body often can give excellent results, and in this case, it was precisely what Roseanne needed to get over the hump.

Roseanne has subsequently had more OOBEs utilizing the same method and suggestions. On most of these occasions, she has stayed around her room. After the first experience, she apparently felt much more comfortable about the whole thing. Her series of out-of-bodies culminated in her having an OOBE in which she no longer felt it necessary to remind herself that she was safe; she knew that she was. During this experience, she ventured out of her window for the first time and flew around her neighborhood.

DEMONS, DRAGONS, AND OTHER UNINVITED GUESTS

Another fear some people have is meeting unfriendly spirits—demons or the like—while outside the body. This brings up some interesting issues. Since you create your reality through your thoughts, if you believe strongly in such spooky creatures, you conceivably could manufacture them and then meet your own creations. They will not really be demons, of course, because demons per se do not exist. They will have no power over you, since it is always you and your own ideas, thoughts, and emotions that determine your experience—no matter what dimension you find yourself in. If you ever encounter such a situation, simply tell yourself that you create your own reality and that you are safe; then wish your "unfriendly" visitor well and go about your business.

Jane Roberts describes an OOBE in *The Seth Material* in which a "big black thing, like a bloated, blurred human form" attacked her, and 'she more or less ran back to her body.'[1] Later Seth explained that Jane had created the creature with her own fears and had set up the experience so that she could sort of fight it out with what she believed to be the evil or negative elements of herself. Seth explained that, from a larger perspective, evil does not exist. The creature Jane created was not evil but a product of her belief. Once Jane withdrew her energy from the newly created being, it would no longer have any reality for her. (It would, however, continue on its own. Nothing that is created is ever extinguished. Any beings to which we give life with our thoughts will go on to learn and grow as all beings do.) Seth further suggested that since evil, in greater terms, does not really exist, Jane would be safe in her out-of-body travels. It was, however, important for Jane to remember that evil does not really exist. Seth recommended that Jane use the phrase "May peace be with you" if she ran into any such creations of her own or others.

Sometimes you can spook yourself out during an OOBE even when there is absolutely nothing around to fear. Here's one of my own experiences along these lines:

I floated out of my body in my bedroom. A friend was there guiding me and said, "The window." I proceeded to float through the window. I saw the image of a woman floating outside. I went into the house into another room, just floating around, and realized I could move by will. I was trying to remember something in the other room as proof. Then for no apparent reason, I started to think about demons. I worked myself up and became frightened. I didn't see anything scary, though; it was all in my head. I closed my nonphysical eyes, and then I couldn't open them. I felt an oppressive weight. Then I remembered that I create my own reality and that there was nothing to be afraid of. Instantly, everything was all right again. I felt crackling electrical energy, and I decided to stop and calm down. I returned to my physical body.

An individual's beliefs about the safety of practicing OOBEs is often intertwined with his or her fundamental belief systems in such areas as good and evil and personal power. If you do not feel safe about your normal, everyday reality, it's quite likely that you won't feel safe about gallivanting around the universe without a physical body. If you think that the physical world is rampant with evil, that belief is likely to carry over to your feelings about nonphysical experience. Whatever the reason, if you don't feel safe about inducing OOBEs, you probably won't allow yourself much slack for doing them.

Generally, if an individual is filled with fear, is depressed, or sees the world as a place riddled with evil, it may be better for him or her to postpone the inner journeys we have been discussing until these issues are addressed and a more positive mental climate is achieved. Nonphysical reality is so thought-responsive that an extremely negative frame of mind can result in experiences that will serve only to reinforce the "negativism."

THE ALLEGED EXISTENCE OF A SILVER CORD

One more concept I would like to touch on is that of the silver cord, which is mentioned in some OOBE literature. Presumably, this cord connects your astral body to your physical one and can stretch infinitely to accommodate you in your travels. It has been said that when an individual is ready to die this cord will somehow become severed. Upon hearing this theory, some people become frightened that their silver cord might be accidentally cut during an OOBE. This is just the sort of alarmist thinking to avoid.

I have never even seen a cord while out-of-body. Some people have seen a cord while out-of-body, and some have not. I don't believe there is any danger of not coming back, cord or no cord, for the reasons already mentioned. In fact, I believe that the silver cord is probably a comfortable way of interpreting a connection between the roving consciousness and the physical body and is therefore created by some people when they are having an OOBE.

That's why it's so important to be what I refer to as a "freelancer" in your inner explorations. Some people who travel out-of-body fail to understand how their own limiting concepts are inextricably connected to what they experience. These concepts can be anything from irrational fear to popular dogma. If you go into an occult bookstore, for example, and read up on metaphysics, sooner or later you'll run into limiting belief systems that prescribe strict rules for inner exploration. It is important to realize that each person's experience in both physical and nonphysical reality is unique and directly reflects his or her own belief systems. Therefore, I recommend that would-be astral explorers avoid any rigid belief systems about the OOBE and proceed with open minds.

When I used to listen to Seth at Jane Roberts's classes, I heard him encourage us to feel confident about trying OOBEs. In fact, in all the years that I knew Seth I don't remember him saying anything frightening or negative about the OOBE. In a recently published book that contains some of the earlier Seth sessions, however, I did come across some rare "precautions" from Seth. In this book, *Seth, Dreams and Projection of Consciousness*, he discusses the different forms or stages of consciousness in which we may find ourselves while out-of-body. The form or stage of consciousness that is most difficult to achieve and maintain involves those travels most divorced from physical reality. Seth points out that images you encounter in such travels are "no more hallucinations" than are physical objects in your room. He states that to avoid danger it's important to "respect the reality in which they exist. . . . You are safe as long as you do not meddle. You may explore, and freely, and that is all."[2]

This is generally good advice, but it is not intended to reinforce a fearful attitude toward the OOBE. Simply have respect wherever you go, and you can feel free to play and fly around to your heart's content.

I once woke up in the middle of the night feeling a strange and powerful energy in my body and in the room. It was so overwhelming that I became frightened. I mentioned the experience to Jane Roberts in the following week's class. At one point, Seth abruptly turned around to me and said, "You will find yourself relaxing about inner reality as you often relax about outer reality. There is no difference, you see. You do not get terrified every time you cross a street, though there is traffic, so there is no need to become frightened when you are walking down some quiet, inner, country road where the only traffic is your own."

6
RENOVATING YOUR MENTAL CLIMATE
FOR OOBEs

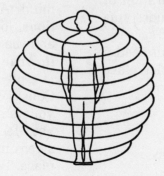

What follows is a series of exercises designed to address specific belief systems that are relevant to our work with OOBEs. I've provided questions to aid in the examination of your beliefs in several areas, as well as exercises for restructuring and altering beliefs, where necessary.

This work will take a bit of time and effort. For many, however, the alteration of limiting mental and emotional attitudes surrounding the OOBE will be the key to success. For most of these exercises you will need a notebook, pen, or pencil and a quiet place where you will not be disturbed.

EXPLORING BELIEFS THAT CAN AFFECT YOUR ABILITY TO INDUCE OOBEs

Exercise 2: Examining Relevant Beliefs

Procedure: Get comfortable. Take several long, slow, deep breaths and clear your mind. After reading through these directions, look at the first subject area below and the questions that immediately follow it. Write out the questions in your notebook in a place designated for that subject area. Consider the questions in your mind. Let your answers come from your thoughts and your feelings. Then start writing your answers in your notebook in the designated place. Take your time. There is no hurry. Be honest with yourself. Try to examine the full range of your beliefs in the area. If you discover that you hold conflicting ideas in a certain area, write down both sides. Let your thoughts flow, and write as much as you want. Take as much time and paper as you need to be thorough. Go at your own rate. If it takes several sittings to cover all of the areas, that's fine. If you breeze through them in a couple of hours, that's fine too—as long as you have honestly examined the full range of your thoughts in each area.

When you are finished with the first subject area and questions, clear your mind and proceed with the next. Continue until you have covered all of the areas.

Subject Area 1:
THE RETURN TRIP

Are you at all uneasy about leaving your body because you think you might wind up not coming back? Elaborate and explain your thinking.

Subject Area 2:
DEGREE OF DIFFICULTY

In general, how easy or difficult do you believe it is to induce OOBEs? Explain.

Specifically, how easy or difficult do you feel it's going to be for you to induce fully conscious OOBEs? Why do you feel this way?

Subject Area 3:
PREREQUISITE TALENT

Do you believe that doing OOBEs requires some sort of talent? Explain.

To what degree do you believe you have what it takes to become an astral adventurer?

Subject Area 4:
FEELING SAFE

How safe do you feel in your life? Elaborate.

Do you feel that the world is a threatening place?

Specifically, what are you afraid of in your world?

Subject Area 5:
SAFETY AND OOBEs

How safe do you feel about leaving your body?

Do you feel that leaving the body might be dangerous in any way? Elaborate.

Subject Area 6:
OUT OF BOUNDS

To what degree do you feel that deliberately inducing OOBEs is a natural or unnatural activity? Explain. Is there any doubt in your mind about the wisdom of tampering with this stuff? Explain.

Subject Area 7:
DESIRE

Just how much do you really want to have these experiences?

How strong is your desire?

Why do you want to leave your body?

Subject Area 8:
VALUE

How important do you think this work is?

How do you rate the value of this work compared to other work in your life?

Specifically, why do you think this work is important?

Subject Area 9:
COMMITMENT

How willing are you to give this work some priority in your life?

Are you ready to commit time and energy to working with OOBEs?

Just how much priority are you willing to give this project?

Subject Area 10:
GOOD AND EVIL

Describe your ideas about good and evil.

Do you believe there are evil forces out there that we should worry about?

How might your beliefs about good and evil affect your upcoming work with OOBEs?

Subject Area 11:
OWNING YOUR POWER

What do you believe about your power to create your reality?

In what areas of your life do you feel powerless?

To what degree do you feel you own your

power and can use it to bring what you want into your life?

Subject Area 12:
OTHER LIMITING BELIEFS

Write down any other limiting beliefs or issues that come to mind when thinking about doing OOBEs.

Exercise 3: Identifying Restricting Beliefs

The next step is identifying beliefs that either are obviously limiting or could be improved upon. For this purpose, use your answers to the questions above and any other insights or intuitions that surface. Here are some examples of typical limiting beliefs:

- It's not easy to induce out-of-body experiences.

- If I leave my body, maybe I'll get lost and never be able to find my way back.

- I've never been particularly psychic, so I doubt I'll be much good at this either.

- We probably should all be staying put in our bodies where we belong.

Procedure: Write out the title of each subject area at the top of a sheet of paper, one subject per page. Starting with the first subject area, read through your responses to the questions. On the corresponding sheet of paper, write out a simple statement expressing your belief in that area as clearly and concisely as possible. Since there are several questions in most areas, you may need more than one statement to cover your beliefs in certain areas. If you hold conflicting ideas, write down both. The idea, however, is to clearly identify your beliefs in each area and try to clarify and crystallize them in one or two plain-language statements.

CUSTOM DESIGNING YOUR MENTAL ENVIRONMENT

In this section you will formulate affirmations and visualizations that you will use to alter your old beliefs. The idea, of course, is to choose new beliefs that will correspond to what you want to achieve with OOBEs. In the case of certain obviously limiting attitudes, you may wish to start focusing on a new belief that is more or less the direct opposite of the old one. In other cases, the change may be more subtle. You may simply need to adjust your old idea so that you can stretch to your next level of development in that area.

The affirmations you will be designing are concise forms of the beliefs that you want to accept. They are belief statements that you can use during self-hypnosis-type exercises. When designing an affirmation, it's very important to select a belief that truly represents the next stage in your growth process in that area. If your new belief will not allow you enough growth—is not enough of a stretch for you—the affirmation may actually bore you. On the other hand, if you choose a new belief that is such a great stretch for you that you don't really believe it is possible to achieve, it may be difficult for you to truly accept it. Therefore, choose a belief that is as much of a stretch as you can handle for now. You can then proceed to stretch further when you update your affirmation at a later date.

When you change your beliefs, it's important that you understand why your old beliefs were limiting and see the mistakes you were making in your thinking. Jot down some reasons why you think the new belief is or can be true for you and why the old one isn't. Think

it through. This way, when you start to focus on your new affirmation belief exercises, you will be supporting your position with logic and sound reasoning; this will help you accept the new belief.

We already discussed a few of the twelve subject areas in prior chapters. I have a few more comments about some of the other subject areas before we get down to the actual work of creating affirmations and visualizations.

Degree of Difficulty: You will probably experience the exact amount of difficulty inducing OOBEs that you expect to encounter. Therefore, your affirmation belief exercise should move you toward expecting little or no difficulty.

Prerequisite Talent: Facility in inducing OOBEs has far less to do with talent than with the practitioner's attitudes and determination. Although some people may be talented in the area, talent is *not* a prerequisite. The ability to leave the body is an *innate* human potential. Developing this potential is the same as developing any other skill: 1 percent inspiration and 99 percent perspiration.

Feeling Safe: In Chapter 5, we discussed feeling safe about leaving your body. What about feeling safe in your day-to-day world? This can also impact on your OOBE work. If you have a lot of anxiety in your day-to-day consciousness, this anxiety may be translated into fears about leaving the body. You may not even be able to pinpoint what you are afraid of but feel that you are simply afraid of the unknown.

Feeling safe in your world is important not only for work with OOBEs but for your overall spiritual fulfillment. Feeling consistently threatened leads to the curtailment of creative energy. It's true that we are often bombarded by newspapers and TV programs that constantly try to tell us how powerless we are to affect events in a dangerous world. We do not, however, have to buy this bill of goods. When you understand that you have the power to create a personally safe reality through the artful use of your focus of attention, you can tune in to a mental climate that will promote the growth of your being. Therefore, if you feel powerless or threatened in your day-to-day life, it is important to remind yourself that you have the power to create a reality of personal safety. Designing and using an affirmation belief exercise to this effect will help you in your OOBE work and provide numerous other benefits. A sample affirmation in this area would be: "I create my reality, and I am absolutely safe from all harm forever."

Desire and Commitment: For many people,

the kind of work we have been talking about involves a considerably different use of their consciousness. Getting the ball rolling may require some persistence. If you fuel your desire, you will increase your chances for success. The questions asked in these subject areas were meant to help you gauge your current desire and commitment. Desire is not static. Using affirmations and visualizations, you can amplify the level of your desire. The idea is to get as excited and pumped up about this work as possible. The intensity of your desire and commitment will bring you the results that you want. A sample affirmation in these areas might go something like this: "I'm really excited about out-of-body experiences. I am 100 percent committed to working with out-of-bodies and I practice every day."

Good and Evil: I believe it is very important to understand that for adventures both out of and in the body, there is really no such thing as evil. What we perceive as evil effects is the result of spiritual and mental "illness." Believing that it is OK to dominate and hurt others or to rape the environment is a form of such illness. In these terms, the planet as a whole is somewhat ill. This does not mean, however, that humankind is *fundamentally* inclined toward evil. Those who come to that conclusion are falling prey to the classic error that perpetuates the overall disease. The "illness" is really a lack of understanding, a misuse of energy by individuals at a certain point along their path of growth and development.

It is extremely important to realize that what you are is fundamentally good; so are humankind and the universe in which we exist. This attitude will lead to your treating yourself and others with love and respect, whether in or out of the body. It will also lead you to understand that there is nothing you need to fear in your out-of-body travels.

Owning Your Power: You will be attempting to use the power of your thoughts and imagination to achieve success in the specific area of inducing out-of-body adventures. Belief that you indeed possess this power will enable you to more fully harness it.

Exercise 4: Formulating Affirmations and Visualizations

Procedure: For this exercise, you will need the twelve pages with your crystallized beliefs. Begin with the first subject area. Look at your belief statement. Use your intuitions and intellect to decide whether this belief is still serving you. If you feel that the belief is limiting, can be improved on, or is simply no longer in line with what you want to accomplish, proceed as indicated. If you are totally satisfied with your current belief in the area and the results it will continue to bring you, there is no need to change it. Go on to the next area. In the areas in which you do wish to make a change, proceed as follows.

In your mind, start to formulate a new belief that will replace the old one in the area. Think about it for awhile and then, on the same sheet of paper, write out a simple statement that expresses the new belief. This is your affirmation. Custom design the statement so that you feel comfortable with it. Experiment with the wording. Write out several versions until you get the one that feels right.

One important thing to note here is that in general affirmations should be stated in the present tense. For example, suppose you currently believe it's difficult for you to induce OOBEs. Some possible affirmations for countering this belief may go something like this:

- It is easy for me to have out-of-body experiences.
- I now have several out-of-bodies every month (or week).
- I induce out-of-body experiences routinely and effortlessly.

After you have decided on the wording of your belief affirmation, write out the final wording.

Now think of an image or visualization you can use with your affirmation. You can create one mental image, like a photograph, that expresses the essence of your belief affirmation. Or you may want to use a mental movie of sorts, with events that unfold. Either way, try to crystallize your visualization into a clear, powerful image of what you want to create. You can use a literal visualization or a symbolic one. For example, you may want to use the image of yourself floating out of your body in your bedroom as one of your visualizations. Or you could use the image of an eagle soaring over the mountains instead.

There are no strict rules here. Everyone will do his or her own thing with these exercises. In some areas, you may not wish to use a visualization. It's perfectly OK to use just an affirmation if you feel it fits better for you in a specific area. The same applies to using visualizations without affirmations. Some people work better with images and others with verbal statements. It's a good idea to use both, though, if it feels right. In conjunction, the affirmation and visualization reinforce each other and make for a more potent exercise. Whatever affirmations or visualizations you come up with now you can change whenever you wish. It's a good idea to adjust them as you go along anyway.

Here's an example of a simple visualization you could use to reinforce the concept that OOBEs are safe and you need not worry about the return trip:

Imagine you are now slipping back into your body after having just completed an out-of-body experience. See yourself doing this in your mind. It is effortless to move back into your physical body. Imagine that you are feeling totally safe, secure, and excited about writing down what you have just experienced.

Here's another example. Suppose you feel that inducing OOBEs may be an unnatural or unwholesome activity. Along with an affirmation for countering that suggestion, you might try a visualization portraying the OOBE as a natural thing to do. It might go something like this:

Imagine that everyone frequently leaves the body in the dream state, without knowing it. See this in your mind. Visualize millions of people peacefully leaving their bodies every night and unconsciously traveling to the inner dimensions of their beings. Imagine the universe or your higher self (or whatever term works for you) approving of your efforts to bring conscious awareness to this perfectly natural dimension of your being.

When you have come up with a visualization for the first subject you are working on, write it below the corresponding affirmation. Continue the above procedure for each subject area you decided to work on until you have a final affirmation and visualization for each.

When you have finished, take a new sheet of paper and put the heading "OOBE Affirmations and Visualizations" at the top. On this sheet, write out the final versions of all the affirmations and corresponding visualizations you have been working on, skipping a couple of lines between each. You will use this sheet in the next exercises.

In the next chapter, we will focus on how to use your affirmations and visualizations.

7
USING AFFIRMATIONS AND
VISUALIZATIONS FOR OOBEs

This chapter will cover a simple method for using affirmations and visualizations to effectively alter your belief systems. If you truly allow yourself to accept the belief that you can leave your body easily and that it is safe to do so, then that is the reality you will create. Remember: Each individual can choose to focus on and accept whatever beliefs he or she wants.

It is pointless to say that you can't change your beliefs because of past experience or what your reasoning mind has concluded about reality. Once you know how to do it, changing beliefs is not hard unless you deliberately resist yourself. If you don't allow yourself to reprogram certain beliefs, at least be aware that you are the one making that decision.

If you are not yet willing to accept the new beliefs you selected in the last chapter, you will probably come up with excuses for not doing the upcoming exercises on a regular basis. You may feel that you are giving up your rationally based mode of operation to accept a new belief before you have any physical evidence supporting it. But if thought creates experience—*and it does*—a new mode of operation is in order.

I am therefore now going to suggest that you really dive into this work and let yourself go. Put aside your doubts for now, and proceed to hypnotize yourself into a frame of mind that will be conducive to what you want to achieve. You don't have to completely obliterate your doubts—just put them on the shelf for awhile.

Don't worry; if at any point you don't like your new handiwork, you can always hypnotize yourself back into believing your old beliefs. Once you realize that beliefs are your playthings, you will be free to do with them as you will.

As a true explorer, trust that what you are doing is important. You are involved in a worthy endeavor, a much-needed exploration of unknown areas of reality. Allow yourself to get excited! Fuel your desire!

Exercise 5: Using Your Affirmations and Visualizations

If you are already familiar with affirmation or visualization techniques, you need only apply them to the new beliefs you have developed for your OOBE work. Following is an example of a simple affirmation/visualization exercise.

Procedure: Set aside a time each day to do your mental work. Find a quiet spot where you can sit undisturbed. Take a few long, slow, deep breaths, and tell yourself that your mind is relaxing. Try to clear your mind of all thoughts and worries. If you want, listen to some relaxing music for a few minutes as you clear your mind.

Take the sheet of paper containing the final versions of your affirmations and visualizations. Start with your first affirmation and begin to speak it, either aloud or in your mind. Say it with feeling, and feel what you are saying. Deliberately allow yourself to *believe* what you are saying as you say it. During the exercise you are to "pretend" that what you are saying is *already true*. Let yourself get into it. Keep your focus of attention exclusively on the topic at hand. Repeat the statement over and over, and then begin using your visualization if you have one. Imagine it as vividly as you can. If you are visualizing something or situation that you want, imagine that you have already achieved your goal.

Even if you have no set visualization, you can use your imagination freestyle. In your mind, see the event you want to happen actually occurring. See yourself, for example, moving effortlessly out of your body, and *feel* the exhilaration and excitement accompanying your success. If appropriate, let yourself produce the emotional equivalent of whatever you are working on. For example, suppose you are working on changing your beliefs about safety when leaving the body. As you verbally tell yourself that it is safe to leave your body and imagine yourself doing so, you can also deliberately produce a feeling of safety during the exercise.

When you have completed your first exercise, proceed with the second, then the third, and so on until you are finished. There is no particular amount of time required. Sometimes, particularly if I am working on several areas, I will take only a minute or two on each one. Other times I will take between five and fifteen minutes for a specific area. But I rarely spend more than ten minutes on any one exercise. Generally, a few minutes are all that is required for each area, and anything over fifteen minutes in one area is unnecessary. I often do about eight different affirmations in less than twenty minutes. Experiment with what works best for you.

This type of exercise can be extremely potent. It is a practical application of power that can be used to literally change the course of your life. You've got nothing to lose by giving it a try. It is applicable for conscious creation in any area.

Some important tips: When sitting down to do your exercises, realize that spending a few minutes imagining something accomplishes work. When you direct the power of your imagination, you are harnessing the awesome creative forces of nature and putting them to work for you.

Consistency in using such exercises is extremely important—this is where many people get stuck. Because this kind of work may appear to go against the grain, some people have trouble being disciplined about doing it. It's important to make a habit of doing your mental work. Do your exercises every day for awhile. Don't miss a day. Later on, if you skip a day or two, it won't matter. Remember to feel free to update and change your exercises whenever you have reached a goal or simply feel like adjusting them.

You do have the power to bring what you want into your life! Do your OOBE affirmations and visualizations for a week or so prior to using the induction techniques in Chapter 10. Continue doing your mental work every day throughout the period you are working on inducing OOBEs. If new issues arise during your work, use the tools you have acquired to examine your beliefs about the issue and to reshape your ideas as needed.

Fred, one of my workshop participants, is an example of someone who used affirma-tions effectively to help to induce an OOBE. A description of his experiences follows:

When I joined Rick's out-of-body class, I con-sidered myself one of the common folk to whom nothing out of the ordinary ever happens. This was in itself a belief that had to change. The purpose of the class was for each of us to achieve some sort of out-of-body ex-perience within the five-week duration. The pressure was on.

It was the night before the second-to-last class when I finally got a shot at it. I had been using affirmations to change my beliefs about OOBEs in general and the supposed difficul-ties surrounding the mysterious process. One suggestion I was using was simply, "I have out-of-body experiences easily and with great lucidity." That night when I went to bed, I began to use relaxation techniques and deep breathing. I gave myself OOBE induction sug-

gestions [discussed in Chapter 10].

I was relaxed and resting for awhile when I felt a tingling sensation start at the back of my neck and work its way down until my whole body was tingling. It grew in intensity. This had happened to me before, but I never knew what to do with it. Something Rick had said in one of the classes helped me to identify this as a chance to get out. So I kept on concentrating on rising. I tried to be playful about it. Then I felt myself "lock in," and I started to rise. It seemed almost too easy to believe. I was as aware and as alert as I'll ever be.

I began to feel frightened. I heard voices saying to me, "Danger, danger." I knew this was just my own fears, though, and my desire for the experience was too strong to let this stop me. I started giving myself all kinds of positive suggestions, like "I have power, and I'm safe," etc.

I continued to rise. I could no longer feel the mattress cushioning my back or hear the radio I had left on very softly at my bedside. I reached a certain point, and the rising stopped. I started to move forward. I started rolling and tumbling in the air until I finally gained some control. I thought to myself that it must have looked pretty funny. I felt like someone who didn't know how to swim who was thrown into the water and started floundering only to find that the water was only waist high.

I was having fun. The sensations were fabulous. I was totally aware of what was happening, and the sensations were so overwhelming that they're hard to describe. After I regained control of my movement, I didn't see anything familiar anymore—just colors and shapes that I was passing through. I kept on moving, and the intensity of the experience continued.

I felt satisfied and victorious. But enough was enough. I had accomplished what I wanted, and I wanted to return to my body and bed. With all the confidence of an experienced pilot, I easily returned to my body, much to my amazement. I felt myself ease into my body and fit in just right. I just seemed to know how to do it. I wanted to get up right away, but I had to wait a few seconds before I could move. Finally, I got up, and it was over. I had so much energy that I couldn't sleep for the rest of the evening.

I was never asleep or in a dream state when this happened. Maybe I was just entering the hypnagogic state, but I stress I wasn't asleep. I was fully alert the whole time. The whole experience was like a roller coaster ride.

What I can achieve from this point on is entirely up to me. What was most important is that I proved to myself that these things don't just happen to the other guy. I look forward to repeating the experience, meeting my inner self, and growing as much as I can with this ability because now I know it's possible.

8
DREAM WORK

The easiest techniques I know for inducing OOBEs involve projection while the body is either asleep or in a state "close to" sleep. Shortly, we will focus on simple methods of accomplishing this. There is some preliminary work with dreams, however, that for many will be a prerequisite for taking full advantage of the techniques that will be presented. For those of you who already work with dreams, some of this will be a review.

Dreams are, quite simply, a natural doorway to the inner dimensions of your being. In the dream state, we travel each night to deep levels where we drink from the fountain of energy and knowledge, which forever sustains our eternal and constantly growing identity. We usually remember little of these deeper excursions because they reach into dimensions of experience that are quite different from the physical world we know so well. Sometimes the dreams we remember are our own attempts to translate this deeper wisdom into a physical play that we can understand.

I believe that, in the dream world, we often visit the past and the future. We communicate with other parts of our beings. We communicate with reincarnational selves, comparing notes, exchanging information, and moving through time as easily as our physical bodies breathe. We receive instruction from our inner selves, the greater selves of which we are a part. And to the degree that we are open to such information, we can facilitate the transfer and incorporation of this learning into our physical lives.

Dreams can be used for many purposes, including problem solving, examining beliefs, gaining understanding about current life situations, promoting health and healing, getting in touch with repressed emotions, and lots more. To take full advantage of this resource, however, it is important to give our dreams the attention they deserve.

I believe that our dreaming selves are just

as valid as our physical selves. They are a portion of ourselves. The dreaming self and the physically oriented self are both parts of our greater identity—an identity that inhabits many dimensions. The dreaming self and the waking self are intimately connected. They are on a continuum of being and are not really separate. They are the same Self, two sides of the same coin but existing in different dimensions. Following is a description of an out-of-body experience I had in which it seemed as if I merged with some of these other parts of my being:

I found myself sitting at a table in a room I did not recognize. At the table were several people, including myself. I was completely alert, and I knew that I was outside my physical body. I was fascinated by how totally real everything looked and felt. This room felt as real as any I had ever sat in. I was myself and knew that I was myself, and yet I was some-how something more. It felt as if I had merged with another, larger aspect of myself. I began to have a discussion with the people at the table about the portion of myself that inhabited normal physical reality. The discussion revolved around my physical self's behavior and characteristics. The self I had merged with in this state seemed to have access to a more enlightened and knowledgeable perspective than the one I normally possessed. It seemed to know a lot of stuff that I didn't; but now that we were together, some of its knowledge seemed available to me. I was not separate from this self. It was me. It was strange indeed to be sitting at a nonphysical table that felt as physical and as solid as any on earth and to hear myself calmly describing and analyzing my normal physical self with a level of insight that seemed to easily exceed what I was used to.

I believe that in the above experience I

merged with my dreaming self. I believe that self is alive and well and living in valid dimensions of experience that we all visit every night. I believe that its existence and experience continues, even when we are awake in the normal physical world. With a little practice, you can learn to bring your waking consciousness with you into the sleep state and thus merge with your "dreaming self," increasing the flow of information between the inner and outer worlds.

The world of our dreams is often considered to be more or less a figment of our imaginations. Instead, it is a pathway of utmost importance—a pathway we were meant to use to discover the full dimensions of our own identities. It is a road that leads to the countless dimensions of reality that will someday be our permanent playground.

Dreams provide the waking self with invaluable information that we often utilize whether or not we remember our dreams. The information may show up at any point of the day as an intuition or insight. In addition, the dream state is part of the mechanism by which we create our lives. It is here that the awesome interconnections and logistics are worked out, which enables you to draw specific events into your life in accordance with your beliefs and in concert with the many other people whose realities all "interface."

If your day-to-day focus is fearful or negative, it is likely that your dreams will reflect this theme. Individuals who find themselves in this predicament can greatly benefit by restructuring their patterns of thinking in order to change the tone of their physical days as well as their dreams.

Dreams can sometimes help you out of depressions by communicating knowledge to you on a deep, emotional level. Here is an example from my journals of a dream I had about twelve years ago, when I was feeling depressed:

In the dream I was feeling depressed about my life and work. I was watching a performance. The performance was going to express two different attitudes, or modes, of operating. The first attitude expressed involved a man who was complaining about everything. He felt that his life and his work were a drag. The second attitude, or mode, of operating was expressed by a man singing an extremely exuberant song. The song was about a man who totally loved living. He loved to work. The song went on to say that every new job or apprenticeship was a joyous and great experience. And then the singer started interacting with the huge audience that was watching his performance. He sang out the words "And God has got His day," and the whole audience sang back, "And God has got His day." After two or three times he sang out, "And I've got mine." The song was extraordinarily beautiful and powerful. The last line was "Treat yourself with the respect that you deserve." I was moved to tears.

When I woke up, my mood had completely changed. The dream had effectively communicated to me on an intuitive level that every day of every person's life is unique, precious, and magnificent. Having many such dreams can literally change the course of your life. If you do not remember and record such dreams, however, it diminishes your capacity to take full advantage of them.

The flow of information between the inner and outer selves can be greatly enhanced by a deliberate attempt to work with dreams. In addition, working with dreams leads directly to skills that facilitate the induction of OOBEs. Here is a general outline of how to proceed. First, develop a habit of remembering, recording, and interpreting your dreams. Then experiment a little with controlling your dreams. This sets the stage for *lucid dreaming* (dreaming in which you realize you are in a dream) and the effective use of OOBE induction techniques. There are no strict rules, so make your own way and go at your own pace. We will begin with a program for working with dreams.

RECORDING YOUR DREAMS

When you make the effort required for recording your dreams, you are making a statement about them. You are saying that you feel they have value. This change in attitude and behavior automatically sets in motion wheels that will lead to greater communication between your physical and nonphysical selves.

Before you can record your dreams, you must remember them. Some people remember their dreams as a matter of course, and others do not; but we *all* dream every night. In any case, it is usually a simple matter to remember dreams by using suggestion.

Prior to sleep, simply repeat any of the following suggestions (or your own version) several times, in your mind or aloud:

- I am going to remember my dreams.

- When I wake up in the morning, I am going to remember my dreams and write them down.

- I am going to wake up right after a dream and remember it.

- I am going to wake up right after the most important (or most fun, or most exciting, etc.) dream (dreams) of the evening and remember it fully.

You can write down your dreams directly, or use a tape recorder and write them down later. In either case, however, it is important to get them down on paper so that you can refer back to them. Keep a separate journal or notebook exclusively for dreams and OOBEs (or one for each). There are just a few important points to remember about recording dreams:

• Keep your notebook or recorder within reach of where you are sleeping.

• Upon awakening from a dream, don't get out of bed. Reach for your notebook or recorder, and record the dream immediately.

• Record the dream in as much detail as possible, including how you felt at different points in the dream.

• If any insights, interpretations, or associations come to you as you are recording the dream, record these also. You may immediately sense that the dream is providing you with insight connected with some specific aspect of your day-to-day life.

• If you are just starting out recording your dreams, don't be discouraged if you remember only scraps at first. Write down whatever you can remember, no matter how minute or silly it seems. This will get the flow going.

Using a tape recorder is really convenient, particularly if you wake up in the middle of the night. Offhand I would say you can tape-record your dreams at least four times faster than you can write them down. Of course, you have to write them down later anyhow, so some people will prefer to do so immediately. I have recently taken to typing my dreams from the tape recorder, since my middle-of-the-night handwriting has proven illegible even to me. The use of a tape recorder has enabled me to record dreams in greater detail and in greater quantity.

If you make dreams a priority in your life, you should have no trouble remembering and recording them. It takes some discipline and commitment, but it is well worth it.

INTERPRETING YOUR DREAMS

Interpreting your dreams on a regular basis is not only an invaluable method for obtaining inner knowledge; it is also a way to familiarize the waking consciousness with inner reality and thus promote a favorable climate for out-of-body experiences during the sleep state.

I am a great believer in what I call *"freelance" dream analysis*. This means that you learn, or relearn, how to interpret your dreams based on your own feelings, thoughts, and intuitions.

When I first started interpreting my dreams, I did so according to other people's ideas about what various symbols mean. Later on, I learned that this method is really off the mark since symbols mean completely different things to different people. A bull in a field could represent something frightening to one person, something filled with energy to another, and a McDonald's hamburger to still another. It all depends on how you feel in the dream and on the unique way you and your dreaming self use symbols.

In short, I recommend that you suspend any preconceived notions with regard to dream interpretation; instead, proceed as indicated in the following paragraphs.

Shortly after you have had a dream and recorded it, sit down to read over and interpret it. If you have the time, you may want to jot down your interpretation immediately after recording the dream. Generally, it's a good idea to get to it within a day or two, so that you can still remember it. Some dreams will be so potent that they will be indelibly emblazoned in your memory. Others may be hard to recall clearly unless you get to them within a day.

We assume here that each of us has access to a potent inner source of information that we can draw upon for the purpose of accurate dream interpretation. I am referring to our intuitive voices, the flow of insights and intuitions that is always available to each of us if we listen. When sitting down to interpret a dream, use your intellect *and* your intuition. Ask yourself what the dream is expressing or trying to tell you, and then simply trust your own answer. That last part is quite important. The more you trust your own intuitive/intellectual interpretations, the more skilled you will become at understanding your dreams.

It's important not to be too literal in your interpretations. Suppose, for example, that you have a dream in which your boss is chasing you with an ax. This does not necessarily mean your boss is out to get you. Try to get insights from your dreams about which beliefs and thoughts you have been concentrating on. Your dreams often will point out issues and challenges that are part of your daily life. How you felt during a dream such as the above will give you important clues. For example, if you were frightened during the experience, this might indicate that you have recently been focusing on fearful thoughts. You may feel threatened about your job situation or about your life situation in general. If you regularly have such dreams in which you are being chased or attacked, for example, this may indicate that you need to work in the area of feeling your power and security in your world.

Some dreams do not even need interpretation per se. *Dream appreciation* might be a better term for this genre of dream. In such dreams, you may receive information in an extremely clear and direct fashion. You may simply need to sense whether this information is mirroring certain beliefs or coming from some inner source of knowledge (or both). If you feel you are receiving important pointers from a teacher or from inner portions of your own being, you have only to pay attention to and value such information.

Some dreams allow you to experience emotions you may be repressing to some degree in daily life. In this regard, they can be quite therapeutic. If you cry in a dream, or you find yourself experiencing extreme anger, love, or terror, this may be your way of allowing yourself to express repressed emotions. Of course, if you can identify specific emotions you are repressing on a regular basis, it would be beneficial to work with your beliefs in that specific area.

Frankly, if you have a lot of scary dreams or pent-up emotions, it's not a big plus for your upcoming work with inducing OOBEs. If you are frightened in your daily life, you might interfere with yourself when you try to leave your body. These issues can be addressed using the methods described in Chapters 5, 6, and 7.

DIRECTING YOUR DREAMS

Once you start remembering and recording your dreams, you can begin to manipulate them by programming yourself before you go to sleep. You may wish to program a dream that will give you specific information about a current dilemma. Or maybe you just want to have a dream that will lift your spirits. You can use dreams as a direct source of artistic creations. You can program dreams for guidance or information about practically any topic. The potentials of inner reality appear limitless.

The technique for manipulating your dreams through preprogramming is simple. Basically, you first decide what kind of dream you want to have. Then you come up with a simple suggestion that expresses the essence of the desired dream. Here are some examples:

- Tonight I am going to have a dream that will give me insight about the upcoming decision I have to make.

- Tonight I am going to have a dream that will help me gain insight about my relationship with ———.

- Tonight I am going to have fun in my dream and wake up in a great mood.

- Tonight I am going to have a dream that will give me insight about how I can improve my health.

- Tonight I am going to have a dream that will help me to get back in touch with my energy.

Simply give yourself the suggestion just prior to sleep. It's best to give yourself suggestions *after* your mind has quieted down and you are extremely relaxed. In addition to the verbal suggestion, which you can say aloud or in your mind, it is helpful to use visualization to program your desired dream. Simply imagine the dream happening just the way you want it to happen. Visualize it in your mind as vividly as you can, repeat your suggestions to yourself for a minute or so, and let yourself drop off to sleep. Happy dreams!

9
THE SPECTRUM OF CONSCIOUSNESS:
OOBEs AND LUCID DREAMS

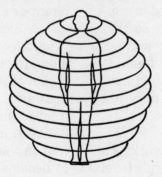

There is a strong connection between dreams and OOBEs. In order to understand this connection, it is helpful to think of the various states of consciousness that human beings experience as being a kind of continuum.

At one end of the continuum are dreams like the ones you can catch yourself creating quickly just before awakening. As mentioned earlier, I believe that in this type of dream we attempt to translate knowledge gained in nonphysical reality into physical terms so that we can bring some of it back to our normal, waking consciousness. This kind of dream is in some ways similar to what we might usually think of as imagination. This does not mean that such an experience has no reality, however.

Again, I believe that the dream world is a natural doorway to the unknown worlds from which we came and to which we will be shortly returning. Sometimes we may find ourselves in dreamscapes with many imaginarylike elements. In certain other dreams, however, I believe we travel to dimensions of existence as real as the physical world, which we usually take for granted as being the only world. Again, this is not to say that dreams with constantly shifting or imaginary-like elements possess no validity, for they do. Different types of dreams could be said to possess varying degrees of reality—literally different gradations of matter and energy.

A *lucid dream* can be thought of as an "upgrade" of a typical dream, one step further along the continuum. A lucid dream is one in which the dreamer realizes that he or she is dreaming. This type of dream often is very intense and vivid. An interesting difference between normal dreams and lucid dreams is that in the latter the dream landscape seems to become more coherent and less dreamlike as soon as the dreamer achieves lucidity.

As we continue to move along our hypothetical continuum, we come to the OOBE.

This state of consciousness can be roughly divided into OOBEs that take place in the physical world and those that occur in nonphysical worlds. OOBEs that take place in nonphysical worlds can be thought of as upgraded lucid dreams.

For the purpose of definition, the main difference between an OOBE in nonphysical worlds and a lucid dream generally seems to lie in the individual's subjective perception. The lucid dreamer thinks that he is in a dream and that what he is experiencing is imaginary. He is either unaware of or unconcerned about the whereabouts of his physical body. The individual undergoing an OOBE, however, is extremely cognizant that he is outside of his physical body, knows where his physical body is, and thinks that what he is experiencing is real.

I believe that in most cases the lucid dreamer is already based outside of the body and simply does not realize it. In other words, most lucid dreams are a form of OOBE. For that matter, I believe that we leave our bodies every night during sleep, whether or not we remember any type of dream.

The lucid dream historically has been an effective pathway to astral travel. Many who have learned how to leave their bodies began by learning how to induce lucid dreams. Converting a lucid dream to an OOBE basically seems to be a matter of realizing that your physical body is sleeping somewhere else and that you are separated from it.

I think what we are really talking about here is the varying degrees of awareness of different states of consciousness. As suggested in Chapter 1, the OOBE itself may fluctuate in its degree of exteriorization. Some lucid dreams may begin with your base of consciousness partially in your body and partially out, and the degree of exteriorization may increase as the experience continues and you focus more intensely on the inner environment. When you realize that you are dreaming and also realize that you are out of your body, the latter realization further upgrades your state of consciousness. It will then be more or less equivalent to other forms of the OOBE, such as floating out of your physical body in your bedroom and consciously witnessing the actual separation. In fact, you can utilize the lucid dream as a launching point from which to return to your physical body and then float out of it in your bedroom if you are so inclined. This technique is described in Chapter 10. Not that you would necessarily want to go rushing back to the physical anyway. In most lucid dreams, your consciousness already has moved its base of operations to the inner worlds. Some of the most exciting and educational excursions outside of the body take place in non-physical reality.

OOBEs generally are more coherent than lucid dreams. In certain ways, OOBEs that occur in physical reality can seem downright "ordinary." Once you're out of your body, you may explore your home or neighborhood and notice that everything is really pretty much the same—that is, except for the fact that you may be flying or walking through walls. Even OOBEs in the inner worlds generally seem more consistent and less dreamlike than lucid dreams. I believe this is due to the particular state of knowing achieved in the OOBE. The inner worlds are thought responsive. Therefore, when you realize that you are out of your body and experiencing a valid reality, that realization in itself allows you to perceive (and create) more clearly.

Robert Monroe calls these inner dimensions Locale II in his book Journeys Out of the Body.[1] He postulates that Locale II is a "nonmaterial environment with laws of motion and matter only remotely related to the physical world." He goes on to say that these locations are inhabited by intelligent beings and that Locale II is the "natural environment of the Second Body" (in other words, the non-physical form used in OOBEs). Since Locale II is where the second body "naturally" wants to go, it will be led there or otherwise wind up there a good deal of the time. In my own experience I have noticed a similar tendency. Even if I started by lifting out of my body in my room and exploring my immediate physical environment, I often wound up in non-physical worlds before the experience ended.

I think it is basically irrelevant whether or not you lift out of your body in your bedroom and then travel to Locale II or instead, simply become lucid in the dream state and then realize you are outside of your body. Both experiences are edifying, though, and worth doing. We will practice techniques covering both of these forms of the OOBE in

Chapter 10. Those who have trouble with the concept of other worlds may want to begin by focusing on OOBEs in which they stick around in physical reality and try to obtain some sort of evidence that they are out.

What some people seem to miss here is the powerful effect of fundamental belief systems on experiences in nonphysical reality. If you have a strong orientation toward believing that the physical world is the only one that should be taken seriously or thought of as "real," this belief will color your experience in a lucid dream or an OOBE. Nonphysical reality is extremely responsive to thought. Rigid assumptions can literally close off an individual to intuitive, direct-knowing experiences about the validity of these nonphysical dimensions.

Some people claim that the OOBE is simply a form of lucid dream. And the lucid dream is generally regarded as just that—a dream—that is, an experience that has no objective reality and exists only in the perceiver's mind. Dismissing OOBEs as just another form of dream is a simple and comfortable way to stay within the bounds of the materialistic assumptions that still hold sway in our culture. It is much more acceptable to tell friends and associates that you once dreamt you flew to someone's apartment than to say you actually left your body (even though you may be able to back up your experience with the fact that you saw something during your excursion that you were later able to verify!). The reality of experience outside of the body is a concept capable of shaking up the very foundations of long-cherished beliefs. It is much easier by far to simply say that OOBEs are unreal and just another form of dream. Nevertheless, OOBEs are real, and we've already seen some scientific support for this concept (in Chapter 1).

There is little agreement about how to precisely define an OOBE. Some people think of the OOBE as an experience in which a person perceives the actual physical world from a viewpoint outside of the physical body. This would include OOBEs in which the individual witnesses the actual separation from the body and is able to see his physical body from the viewpoint of his "astral" body. Others define the OOBE as any experience in which one feels one's mind or point of awareness is outside his physical body whether he is perceiving the physical world or some other dimension of experience. This would include OOBEs that are initiated from the dream state and in which the individual may journey to valid inner ("dream") worlds.

To clarify, we can identify several different forms of the OQBE:

1. Consciously witnessing yourself float out of your physical body and remaining in the physical universe

2. Consciously witnessing yourself floating out of your physical body and then traveling to other dimensions of experience

3. Finding yourself out-of-body without having witnessed the actual separation from your physical body

4. Realizing that you are in a dream and then realizing that you are out of your body

5. Just realizing that you are in a dream (in this case, you are most likely already outside of your body even though you don't know it)

An interesting question to consider here is: Where does normal waking consciousness lie on our hypothetical continuum? This is really a moot point, but I would like to mention that in some ways the OOBE can offer a more complete picture of one's true identity than does normal waking consciousness. Although our day-to-day consciousness seems coherent enough, it is often associated with a limited understanding of the greater context in which we exist. The physical reality we perceive during our normal waking state thus might even be thought of as a dream that we have focused upon too intensely.

The OOBE, it can be argued, often includes an intuitive understanding that existence is not dependent on the physical body, and could therefore be considered an upgrade of our normal waking state. Of course, this knowledge—and some of the other understandings that are seemingly more accessible during an OOBE—can also be achieved during normal waking consciousness, so it would be inaccurate to say it is intrinsic only to OOBEs. In addition, as previously mentioned, some people stifle the potential of the OOBE state with rigid assumptions. Finally, all of the various states of consciousness we have been discussing are artificial divisions made only for the sake of clarity. The dreaming self, the waking self, the OOBE self, the inner self, and the soul are all one, and all attempts to strictly categorize them ultimately will fall short. Let's just say that the relative position of normal waking consciousness on our hypothetical continuum depends on your point of view.

None of this means that people do not sometimes hallucinate while out-of-body; they do. Many people have seen objects, scenarios, and even their own bodies while having OOBEs, only to discover later that their visions contained a few or many imaginary elements. On the other hand, numerous people have reported OOBEs in which they could accurately describe physical scenes and events that could not possibly have been perceived from the standpoint of their physical bodies and the use of their physical senses. You can affect the degree of hallucinatory elements that you encounter while out-of-body by deliberately asking or willing that all

hallucinations disappear. Apparently this type of skill, as well as other fine-tuning abilities, can be improved only through practice.

In our culture, we have been trained to look to the intellect as the only reliable voice. We have blocked off the intuitive knowledge that is our birthright. We have learned to always question intellectually the wisdom we already possess on deeper levels. Learning to trust our own inner knowledge and listen to our intuition is a major step in our spiritual growth. If you really trust your intuition and feelings, eventually you will simply "know" that in most of your lucid dreams you are already out of your physical body. By using this theory as a working hypothesis, you will be able to more easily induce OOBEs from the dream state and open yourself to experiences and knowledge that may otherwise be blocked.

The real art of leaving your body involves learning how to operate effectively wherever you go, whether floating around your bed or traveling in inner reality. There are all sorts of degrees of consciousness that you may experience while outside of your body. In general, you can improve your degree of conscious clarity through practice.

10
SUREFIRE TECHNIQUES FOR GETTING OUT

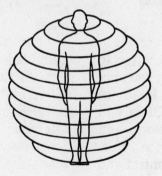

Getting out-of-body could very well be one of the most exciting adventures of your life. If you have made up your mind to do it and will not take no for an answer, you *will* succeed! Remember:

••••●●••••
GETTING OUT IS EASY!
ANYBODY CAN DO IT!
ALL YOU REALLY NEED IS THE DESIRE!
••••●●••••

In some OOBEs you will find yourself in your own bedroom or some other location in the current physical world. In others you may find yourself in a different time or in an entirely different dimension. Some OOBEs will start out in the current physical world and then shift to other dimensions, or vice versa. As you practice, you'll gain more control and become more familiar with the inner terrain.

THE DISCOVERY OF TECHNIQUE #1

There are many different methods and systems for getting out-of-body. Many of them, however, are either ambiguous or over-complicated. The techniques I am going to describe are the simplest and easiest ways I know of to start inducing out-of-body experiences.

My favorite technique is one that I stumbled on accidentally in the early seventies. At that time I was experimenting with altered sleeping patterns. I was sleeping fewer hours at night and taking a nap in the afternoon.

One day, I deliberately woke up at 4:00 A.M., after four hours' sleep, got out of bed, and started reading a book. After about twenty minutes, I found I was having trouble keeping my eyes open. I was feeling extremely relaxed. It occurred to me that I was very close to the sleep state and that this might be an excellent time to try getting out-of-body. So I stretched out in a comfortable easy chair and started to give myself the following suggestion: "I am going to have an out-of-body experience. I am going to let myself drop off to sleep, but I am going to bring this waking consciousness with me wherever I go."

I repeated the suggestion over and over for a minute or so. I then had the out-of-body experience described in the introduction to this book. This marked the first time I was consciously out of my body while still in physical reality. It was also the first time I was able to will myself back to my physical body and see my bedroom through my eyelids.

When I first started using Technique #1, I was unfamiliar with the OOBE literature. Years later, while perusing some OOBE books, I found that others had successfully used similar methods. Technique #1 consists of the following combination of factors:

- The practitioner has recently been asleep.

- The duration of the sleep period has been relatively short (somewhere in the neighborhood of 3½ to 4 hours).

- The practitioner deliberately stays awake for a short period of time before making the OOBE attempt.

- The practitioner makes the OOBE attempt just prior to dawn (see explanation below).

- The practitioner takes advantage of this

auspicious moment by giving himself or herself simple, concise suggestions designed to initiate an OOBE.

I believe this unique combination of factors works well for several reasons. The period of sleep immediately prior to the OOBE attempt produces an energized yet relaxed state. Your body has already been considerably refreshed and so has your consciousness. In addition, since you have recently been asleep, your consciousness seems to still be "close" to the sleep state. It seems that the flow between inner and outer consciousness continues until you fully wake up. Since the immediately preceding sleep period is deliberately kept short, you are less groggy than you would be after sleeping long hours. In addition, your muscles are usually quite impatient for movement after long periods of sleep; muscle relaxation generally is an important element in any OOBE attempt.

Staying awake for a short period just before the attempt seems to stimulate the normal waking consciousness without allowing it to fully wake up and fixate on physical reality. This prepares you for bringing your normally physically focused awareness "across," into other dimensions of experience.

Seth, my former teacher, claimed that the period just prior to dawn is a "high-energy" time of day. In my own experience, I have found this to be true. This does not mean that the above technique will not work at other times of the day, for it will. The predawn period is not an essential element, but it does seem to be a particularly favorable time for movement between the inner and outer worlds. So if you want to have everything possible working in your favor, this is something that can help.

You can do your out-of-bodies anywhere

you are comfortable enough to sleep and have peace and quiet. I started doing my OOBEs stretched out in a comfortable chair. Everyone will have his or her individual preferences here. I found the chair helpful because it established a sort of ritual. Whenever I stretched out in that chair, I expected to go out-of-body. Some people may prefer a completely horizontal position, as in bed; others may find a slightly inclined body position helpful.

Technique #1: Combining Suggestions with Favorable Conditions

With Technique #1, your OOBE generally will be preceded by a temporary loss of consciousness as you drop off to sleep.

1. Plan to sleep about 3½ to 4 hours (no longer) and to wake up approximately an hour before dawn. Set your alarm accordingly.

2. When you wake up, get out of bed, stretch a little, and stay up for a short while. For some people it may work better to stay up just a few minutes; for others a half hour may be just right. Experiment with staying up between five minutes and a half hour until you discover what works best for you.

3. You may want to do something while you are awake, but remember: The idea is to stay in a nice, relaxed mood. You may want to read a book, listen to some music, or do something else that will keep you relaxed. (By the way, if you do read for awhile, read something that will help inspire you in your OOBE attempt. Obviously it would not be helpful to read, say, a scary novel or horror story.)

4. After staying up for five to thirty minutes,

get comfortable and prepare to go back to sleep—but this time expect to have an OOBE.

5. As soon as you get yourself settled, give yourself the following suggestions:

> I am going to have an out-of-body experience. I am going to let myself go to sleep, but I am going to bring this waking consciousness with me wherever I go. I am going to leave my body with full awareness.

Repeat these suggestions, or your own version of them, several times. Then just let your mind drift as you go to sleep. Sometimes you will almost be asleep but then abruptly wake up. Repeat the suggestions each time this occurs.

If things go according to plan, you will temporarily lose consciousness as you fall asleep and then find yourself awake and out-side of your body either in physical reality or inner reality. Another possibility, however, is that you may find yourself still in the body but in the hypnagogic state. The *hypnagogic state* occurs just prior to sleep. In this state, although your body is no longer fully awake, you are not yet fully asleep. You are in between waking and sleeping. Once you learn to recognize this state, you can use it to float right out of your body as described in Technique #2.

Be playful! Have fun! Don't take this too seriously. Just relax and enjoy. You may want to set your alarm clock for thirty to forty-five minutes in case you fall into a normal sleep state. The alarm will wake you up, and you can try again if you so desire. Don't allow yourself to get easily discouraged. You may have to try this technique many times before getting the results you want. Record your experiences immediately after having them.

Technique #1 may require some discipline and commitment if you are used to sleeping seven or eight hours. It is a particularly potent method, however, and is well worth the effort. On evenings when you don't feel like dragging yourself out of bed after just a few hours of sleep, you can still try for an OOBE using one of the following abbreviated variations. Once you get the ball rolling, any of these variations might work for you. Until you do succeed in having a few OOBEs, however, I recommend that you focus your attention on the complete version of this technique as given above.

Abbreviated Variations:

1. Set your alarm for an hour before you would normally wake up. When you wake up, stay in bed, reset your alarm, and then lie back and give yourself the OOBE suggestions mentioned above. Then let yourself go back to sleep.

2. When you wake up spontaneously from a dream in the middle of the night, record the dream and then give yourself the OOBE induction suggestions before going back to sleep. If you do not remember your dream, simply stay awake for a minute and give yourself the OOBE suggestions. Try to energize your resolve to have an OOBE.

3. Simply give yourself OOBE suggestions just prior to going to sleep at night or before a nap.

Technique #2: Floating Out from the Hypnagogic State

Technique #2 focuses exclusively on using the hypnagogic state. The hypnagogic state is an ideal launching pad for OOBEs. In Technique #1, you utilize suggestion and then allow yourself to lose consciousness as you drop off to sleep. In Technique #2, you never really let your consciousness go to sleep—just your physical body. You can go into the hypnagogic state and then lift right out of your body in your bedroom without ever losing consciousness of what is going on. The body itself seems to go into a more or less normal sleep state.

You can use Technique #2 anytime before going to sleep. (You can also use it in conjunction with Technique #1. To do this, simply follow the first four steps of Technique #1 and then proceed with Technique #2.)

1. After you are settled and ready to go to sleep, tell yourself that you are going to catch yourself in the act of going to sleep and then lift out of your physical body. Just be clear about your intent. You are going to let your body go to sleep, but you will remain alert throughout the entire procedure. Tell yourself that you will retain consciousness even while your body is going into the "trance" of sleep. Now,

watching yourself go to sleep is kind of like watching a pot of water boil. Trying to stay too alert may interfere with your efforts. Therefore, a gentle sort of alertness is what is required. Just let yourself relax into sleep and observe the process. The idea is to learn to recognize the rather strange but distinctive sensations you feel as your body moves into the sleep state and stay aware as this unfolds. At a certain point you will realize that you are in the hypnagogic state, the state between waking and sleeping.

A slight variation on this theme is to give yourself the suggestion that you are going to become aware in the middle of the transition to sleep. Instead of "watching yourself," suggest that you will pay attention as soon as you feel your body starting to get numb, and then just let your mind drift. Your suggestions might go something like this:

I am going to have an out-of-body experience. I am going to become alert and aware as soon as I start to fall asleep (or as soon as my body feels numb).

OR

I am going to become alert and aware in the middle of falling asleep, and then I will lift out of my body.

2. Once you succeed in catching yourself in the act of moving through the early stages of sleep, you will be in the hypnagogic state. You will still be in your body, but definitely not in a normal state of consciousness. You may very well feel as though you're paralyzed since you may no longer have control over your physical muscles. There are other, "inner" muscles, however, awaiting your direction. You may feel strange, tingling sensations and hear weird sounds. Your body may feel numb.

After a few times, though, these feelings will become familiar and clue you in to what is going on. You may be able to see right through your eyelids. Just relax and simply will yourself to lift out. This is not difficult to do. You will feel a definite sensation of detaching. Just go with it and move out fast and easy. If you want, you can imagine you are as light as a helium balloon as you will yourself to lift out.

INDUCING LUCID DREAMS AND OOBEs FROM THE DREAM STATE

As mentioned earlier, I believe that in most lucid dreams your consciousness is already based outside of your body. The realization at this point that you are out-of-body seems to shift your consciousness to a state more or less the same as the one you achieve with a lift-out technique, such as Technique #2. You may indeed find yourself in a dreamscape with many imaginary-like elements, but once you realize you are out of your body you can transform the dreamscape and project yourself anywhere you wish. Then again, you may not wish to transform the dreamscape because you may already be in a dimension of experience worth investigating.

Whenever you find yourself in a lucid dream, you can convert it to a consciously experienced OOBE by realizing that your physical body is asleep in bed and you are somewhere else. Simply tell yourself that you are out of your body. Repeat it several times, and hold onto this awareness as you proceed.

The ability to induce lucid dreams or OOBEs from the dream state is a function of many factors, including the creation of a conducive climate of belief, the attention that you pay to your dreams, and your desire and persistence. Once you get going, you will begin to expect to have out-of-body experiences from the sleep state. Thus, you can begin developing a habit of having OOBEs. During periods when you are working on inducing OOBEs, you may find yourself having them spontaneously from the dream state even if you failed during an "official" attempt. In fact, sometimes you can try too hard and interfere with yourself. So it's a good idea to stay light and playful about the whole thing.

One obvious method for inducing lucid dreams is to give yourself a suggestion before you go to sleep. Simply tell yourself that you are going to wake up within a dream and realize that you are dreaming. Remember that you can "convert" lucid dreams into OOBEs.

Technique #3: Strange to the Strange

Probably one of the most common ways people become alert to the fact they are in the dream state is by noticing that something very strange is going on. For example, you find yourself at work, but your desk is on the roof. Or you are in your apartment, but the walls are a different color. There are infinite variations along these lines. The goal is to try to create a mental set in which you clearly intend to recognize these oddities when they occur.

When you are already in bed and about to go to sleep, tell yourself you are going to recognize something strange in your dream and realize that you are dreaming. Then proceed to visualize a sample scenario. For example, see yourself walking around in your home. Suddenly you notice the furniture is completely different. Imagine yourself then realizing that you are in a dream. Then imagine saying to yourself out loud in the dream, "I'm dreaming! I'm in a dream! I'm outside of my physical body!" Say it several times. Imagine that as you say this to yourself your awareness becomes crystal clear. . . .

Then allow yourself to go to sleep.

Technique #4: The Joy of Flight

I believe that in most flying dreams you are already out of your body although you may not even realize you are dreaming. Lucid dreamers often report that flying dreams clued them in to the fact that they were in the dream state. The induction of flying dreams is really a variation of Technique #3. Flying with no visible means of support apparently is strange enough to jar many people into inner wakefulness.

Before you go to sleep, tell yourself that you are going to fly in a dream and realize that you are out-of-body. Then visualize a scenario. Imagine yourself joyfully soaring over mountains and lush valleys or anywhere that suits your fancy. Imagine that as you are flying it suddenly dawns on you that you must be dreaming. This awareness enhances your clarity and your ability to fly. You now have even greater control than before. Imagine yourself flying effortlessly as you tell yourself out loud that you are out of your body! Then let yourself drop off to sleep, and expect to have some fun.

Another variation on the theme of recognizing strange situations is doing so during a false awakening. In a false awakening, you dream that you have awakened even though you are really still asleep. You may even dream that you get out of bed and start writing down your dreams. These experiences may start happening spontaneously as you work with your dreams. Since the scene of the false awakening (your home) is familiar to you, it's an opportune time to notice the strange objects or situations that often show up and thus realize that you must be dreaming. Then, "upgrade" your state of consciousness by telling yourself that you are out-of-body.

Once you realize you are out-of-body and in some "dream" dimension, it's time to have some fun. One place you can travel to is back to your physical body in order to experience a lift-out. Deliberately returning from the inner worlds to your physical body and then floating right out of your body in your bedroom can really knock your socks off! This technique is good practice and exciting, but only one of your options. You may not wish to go back to the physical world just yet but prefer to explore inner reality. We will have some suggestions along these lines in Chapter 11.

Technique #5: From the Inner to the Outer

Technique #5 itself is as simple as can be. Once you have upgraded a lucid dream by realizing you are out-of-body, proceed to tell yourself that you are out-of-body several times in order to intensify the focus and avoid falling back into a lucid or normal dream state. Then tell yourself that you are going to return to your physical body *without* waking up. Simply give yourself this suggestion, and will yourself back to the physical. If you want, you can visualize your physical body as you give yourself the suggestion.

Once you succeed in getting back to your body without awakening, you should be in a situation somewhat similar to the hypnagogic state mentioned earlier. For all practical purposes, though, your body has been asleep for awhile, so this state is probably not identical to the in-between state. Although you may be back in the vicinity of the body, you may feel that you're still not connected or in phase with the physical. You may feel as if you're just kind of floating around inside your own body. If you want to wake up, you can use suggestion to will yourself to do so. If you want to lift out, however, this is a particularly conducive moment. Simply will yourself to float right out in the room. Controlling your movement is something you will get the knack of as you practice. There is a feel to it as you learn to use inner muscles, and it's not hard.

Here is a description of an interesting OOBE resulting from this technique from Carl, a participant in a five-week course I was teaching on OOBEs and dreams:

I was watering the yard near a small house in California when I realized that I was in a dream. I wanted to have an out-of-body, so I put myself back into my physical body. I knew that my body was lying in bed, so I concentrated on my body lying in bed instead of being in the dream. I wound up in my body but still in the hypnagogic state.

I concentrated on the ringing in my ears, which amplified and turned into an energy rushing through my body. I had experienced this before, and it used to scare me; but now I realized from my reading and the class that you can use the energy to just easily lift up out of your body. I opened my astral eyes, and I could see my physical hands and arms stretched out next to me. I remember seeing very clearly my astral hands in front of my face. I was lying in my bed with my eyes closed, and my physical hands were not in front of me; but I was able to see my astral hands stretched out in front, right through my eyelids. So I lifted up out of my body and ended up in a back alley of a building I didn't recognize.

There were two of me standing on a dirt road behind these buildings. [From what happens from this point on, it appears that Carl had been drawn back to a nonphysical realm.] I wanted to go one way, and my other self wanted to go another. I followed him, my other self, for a moment, trying to convince him to go my way, but then he went off in his own direction. Before he left I said, "Let's talk to the first person we see and tell him that we're dreaming."

I went up to an older woman and asked her what she could tell me about what was going on. I was hoping she could help me since I was out-of-body, but she didn't seem to know what I was talking about. So I told her that we were dreaming. She stopped and thought about it and realized it was true. I looked at her face very carefully so I would remember it, and she turned into a younger woman. Then I was talking to someone else. There were strangers around me and also the woman I was talking with before. We both started to tell everyone we saw that we were dreaming because no one seemed to realize it. I told a janitor, and he told someone—and soon there was a huge crowd. I walked up this corridor, and I kept telling everyone I saw that we were dreaming. As soon as they *realized it, they'd start telling everyone else, so we had this huge crowd gathered in front of this big picture window—a great big picture window in this huge mall or business complex. So we all had realized that we were dreaming, and I started leading these affirmations about sending joy and love and understanding. I shouted the affirmations, and we sent them to Russia. I knew that I had taken an afternoon nap and realized that [at this hour] everyone was asleep in Russia, so we could send this message to them. I felt it going telepathically, and I was literally feeling the energy flowing out of my voice and out of the window toward Russia. And there was this beautiful sunset that I could see through this big picture window. I knew that my physical body was actually lying in bed. I was very aware of it, and as I finished the affirmations with the word* brotherhood *and all our voices were rising up in harmony, I opened my phys-*

ical eyes and wrote this all down. It was so powerful. You start to be able to function in that other world, and you realize what power you have.

Of course, some would say that Carl's experience of willing himself back to the physical body and seeing his astral hands through his physical eyelids was just a dream. They would have a hard time convincing Carl of that, however. After practicing for awhile, you should be able to feel and sense the difference between your physical body and a hallucinated version. If you want to check on this yourself, you may wish to set up your own OOBE vision experiments; we will cover these in the next chapter.

MORE LUCID-DREAMING TECHNIQUES

There are many other techniques for inducing lucid dreams, and I would like to include a few more here. Any technique that works for you will help your OOBE work. Once you realize that you are dreaming, it is a short step to also realizing that your physical body is in bed and that you can project anywhere you wish.

In 1983, Paul Tholey reported on his work with techniques for inducing and manipulating lucid dreams.[1] He conducted his work over several years and based his techniques on information gained from experiments with more than 200 subjects. Of the techniques he describes, the one that apparently was most effective was called the *Reflection Technique*. In this technique, the individual develops a "critical-reflective" attitude about his or her current state of consciousness; in other words, the individual frequently questions what state of consciousness he or she currently is in. The idea here is that if you get into a habit of questioning what state of consciousness you are in during the day, you will carry this critical-reflective attitude with you into the dream state. When you ask yourself what your state of consciousness is while dreaming, it is hoped you will realize that you are in a dream.

The question Tholey's participants used was "Am I dreaming or not?" Tholey recommends asking yourself this question at least five to ten times a day. In addition, you should ask yourself the question just before falling asleep and at points during the day that resemble a dream experience (for example, when something surprising happens or when experiencing strong feelings). Tholey suggests that when asking the question you consciously reflect on what has been happening in your immediate past. The reason for this, according to Tholey, is that as soon as you ask a critical question in a dream, the dream generally becomes less bizarre. In other words, even if you have the presence of mind to ask the critical question in a dream, you may look around and conclude that you are *not* in a dream; if you try to remember what happened in your immediate past, though, you may remember unusual experiences or notice a memory lapse, either of which can clue you into the fact that you are in the dream state.

Some of the other techniques Tholey mentions are quite similar to the hypnagogic techniques already discussed. In one, Tholey suggests that you concentrate on the visual images that come into your mind as you are going to sleep and try to retain lucidity as you are passively drawn into the scene. In another, you simply focus on your body as you are falling asleep. When your body feels immobile, imagine that you have another, movable body that can separate from your immobile body. Tholey acknowledges that this technique can produce out-of-body experiences, but he does not believe such experiences are real. Although obviously I disagree with his position, I feel that the techniques described above are excellent.

An interesting technique developed by Stephen Laberge[2] involves counting to yourself in the following fashion as you are going to sleep: "One, I'm dreaming. Two, I'm dreaming," and so on. After awhile, you may find that you are in a lucid dream.

Laberge developed another interesting technique that he calls the *Mnemonic Induction of Lucid Dreams* (MILD).[3] The basic procedure involves waking up in the morning, memorizing a dream you have just had, and then giving yourself the suggestion, "Next time I'm dreaming, I want to remember to recognize I'm dreaming." Then you visualize yourself back in the same dream but imagine that this time you know it's a dream. Then you repeat the suggestion, and imagining, until you are clear about what you are trying to accomplish or until you drop off to sleep.

OTHER TECHNIQUES FOR LEAVING THE BODY

Many other techniques for inducing OOBEs have been put forth over the years. I will mention a few more, but in general I think the ones we already have covered are the easiest and most effective. I recommend concentrating on them for starters, unless you are especially drawn to some other technique.

Hypnosis

There are several audiotapes on the market designed to induce OOBEs using hyp-nosis. The subject is hypnotized and then given suggestions to lift out or imagine himself or herself lifting out of the physical body. You can try this technique, or you can tailor-make your own audiotape. I will not go into self-hypnosis techniques here, but if you are interested, information on the subject is readily available in bookstores.

Relaxation

Some people can induce OOBEs by simply willing themselves out of their bodies during a relaxed state. There are many methods for getting into a relaxed state; you probably already know several, as they have become quite popular. Prior to putting yourself into a state of relaxation, give yourself the suggestion that you are going to leave your body. Then try to will yourself out, or imagine yourself floating out, after you have achieved a relaxed state.

Progressive muscle relaxation (PMR) is an excellent relaxation technique. It consists of alternately tensing and relaxing various muscles in your body. Begin by tensing your toes; hold the tension for a few seconds, then release. Proceed with the entire foot, then calves, thighs, and so on, one part at a time, until you have alternately tensed and then relaxed each portion of your body. A variation of this technique consists of focusing your mind on each part of your body and deliberately relaxing the muscles there. Continue until you have relaxed each part of your body. Once you are in a relaxed state, proceed to try to lift out; or visualize yourself already out and at a different location.

You can also use meditation techniques or rhythmic breathing exercises to get into a relaxed state. These techniques may also help you in entering the hypnagogic state if used just prior to sleep. A participant in one of my recent OOBE workshops used a combination of some of these methods with great success. After lying down, he mentally counted down from twenty to one and directed a different part of his body to relax with each count. Then he utilized a breathing technique to relax further. He breathed in, held his breath for a count of ten, and then released his breath a little at a time as he again counted to ten. (This is quite similar to some yogic breathing techniques.) He performed this procedure several times until his body felt numb. At that point he was able to lift out of his body. He said this technique had worked for him on numerous occasions, noting that it worked best when he was tired but not sleepy.

Needless to say (but I will say it anyway), the techniques presented in this chapter may not work on the first try. Learning how to induce OOBEs is a new skill for most people. As with any other new skill, you will have to practice to get results. Getting out and flying around town, however, is really an easy level to achieve. On the whole, getting to that level of ability is easier than learning tennis but more difficult than learning Parcheesi. Once you find yourself fully conscious out of the body, the possibilities for learning and adventure will be vast. In the next chapter, we will discuss some suggestions for what to do once you're out!

11
THINGS TO DO IN THE ASTRAL WORLD

Let's say you find yourself out of your body. What do you do then? Well, you can wait until you are out and then see what strikes your fancy. That's fine. Or you might want to have a few projects in mind to try once you find yourself floating around somewhere. This chapter includes a few suggested activities to play around with in nonphysical reality.

There are countless worlds and dimensions to explore. There are also widely diverging views and dogmas with respect to nonphysical "geography." I generally recommend doing your own thing and making your own way. Try to keep in mind that you create your own reality according to your beliefs, thoughts, emotions, and imaginings, whether in physical or nonphysical reality.

In my OOBEs, I generally have found myself in some sort of nonphysical equivalent of my physical body. In the OOBE literature, this is sometimes referred to as the *double*. Some people have reported OOBEs in which they were a point of consciousness in space without any type of body. Whether you experience having a body or not may be determined by what you feel more comfortable with. Aside from that, there are various theories about how many different types or gradations of nonphysical bodies exist.

It makes sense to me that people may need different vehicles or forms to accomplish different things, or travel to different dimensions, in nonphysical reality. I think the important thing to realize is that the form you use while out-of-body is a reflection of your state of consciousness. By shifting your consciousness to accomplish something, you shift into the form that has those abilities. For example, I have sometimes found myself out-of-body in a form that seemed too dense to be able to pass through a wall or window. By telling myself I could do it and willing myself to do so, however, I seemed to be able to shift into a "form" that could pass through the wall easily. The shift in consciousness seemed to shift the form or its capacities.

If you actually witness yourself floating out of your body, it's obvious that you are not in your normal physical body. If you find yourself in some nonphysical landscape, however, sometimes it's not so obvious. You may realize that you are out of your body but still want to check to make sure. I have had some extended OOBEs in inner environments that felt so identical to normal reality that I felt compelled to check several times during the experience even though I realized I was out. Sometimes I would try floating or willing something unusual to happen in order to make sure I was not in normal physical reality. Often I would spend time trying to explain to others that they were out of their bodies too. I was not surprised when some did not believe me, because sometimes there really seemed to be no difference at all between inner and outer reality.

As you begin learning how to leave your body, it might take some time to learn how to hold the focus. For awhile you may have brief experiences in which you get out and then wind up back in your physical body after a few moments. Then again, you may get the hang of it relatively quickly. You will be learning to flex your OOBE muscles, and the more you practice, the better you'll get. Whenever you feel you're ready, you can try some of the following suggested activities.

MEETING YOUR INNER SELF

A fun thing to try while out of your body is to ask to meet your inner self. Whether we call it the *soul, higher self, god within, multidimensional self,* or something else, each of us is more than what we usually think we are. In our culture we have generally been taught to disregard or mistrust our own inner wisdom. But our greater identity is always with us, and we are a part of its composition. The wisdom of our greater identity is always ripe for the picking. It communicates to us through the voice of our intuition and our everyday spontaneous inclinations.

Since we are only in the beginning stages of understanding the full extent of our beings, our concepts of the larger self are probably only approximations of the real thing. In other words, your larger self may not meet you in precisely the terms you prefer; you might not get a formal introduction. Your inner self may have its own ideas of how it wants to connect with you. A case in point is a somewhat humorous OOBE I once had in which I attempted to meet my inner self:

I was out of my body and started flying around inside a house. I tried to get out of the house by going through the wall, but I was having difficulty. I noticed a door and decided to go through it the normal way. Outside was lush greenery and paths stretching as far as the eye could see. I thought to myself, "This is where I want to be." Then I had an urge to find my inner self. I called out, "Where is my inner self? I want to find my inner self." Suddenly a bed appeared in front of me. There was someone in the bed, but hidden under the covers. So I went over to the bed and pulled off the cover. There was another cover, so I pulled that one off too, only to find yet another one. No matter how many I pulled off, there were always more covers. When the experience ended, I received an insight that I was ignoring the numerous layers of my larger self. I was looking for one inner self, but the inner self is not structured that way. The inner self is composed of numerous layers of identity.

Here's another example:

I was out of body, and I asked to meet my entity, my inner self. I felt something touch me, very gently at first. It began to touch me all over. This was not a physical touch. This is difficult to describe, but what I had contacted was me, expanding. I felt energy and sensations of my consciousness opening doors into the vast reaches of my multi-identity. I was experiencing my multidimensionality. It was extraordinary, but virtually impossible to put into words.

TEACHERS AND GUIDES

When you have worked with this stuff for awhile, teachers and guides will probably start appearing spontaneously in your lucid dreams and OOBEs. If you want to arrange for such an encounter, try asking for a teacher or guide after you have induced an OOBE. Receiving and bringing clear information back with you may take some practice, however.

Here's an illustration:

I asked for a teacher in an OOBE and, after hearing some strange sounds, a manlike figure showed up covered in purple material. At first I got nervous because it was all too real. Then I calmed down a bit. The figure told me to keep my hands at my sides and follow him. Apparently he was going to pop into some other place just as he had popped up here and expected me to follow him. I couldn't do it. I started getting fuzzy and losing my focus, and he started to lose his patience. He left, and I was unable to follow him.

This type of experience can be a little frustrating, but it's part of the learning process and generally fun anyway. On other occasions I have had conversations with teachers that produced some really excellent information or advice.

INCREASING CLARITY OF AWARENESS

I once had an out-of-body experience in which someone literally pulled me out of my body by the hand:

I flew to Public School 209 in Queens, New York City. This was where I had gone to elementary school and where I frequently returned with friends throughout the years to play basketball. I then proceeded to deliberately increase my clarity. I concentrated on seeing, feeling, and hearing everything as clearly as possible. All of a sudden, my senses seemed to snap together, and in a flash I felt an extraordinary clarity of awareness. I stood for a moment in the schoolyard, feeling enormously energetic and savoring the night air. The effort to bring my senses together had resulted in an extremely pleasurable intensity of aliveness. I could scarcely contain my enthusiasm as I took off like a rocket ship and flew across and out of the schoolyard.

This is an excellent exercise to practice to improve your focus and clarity while out of your body. Simply concentrate your attention and try to intensify your level of sensation and awareness.

FLY ME TO THE MOON

Or why not fly yourself while out-of-body? For all of you who have always wanted to be astronauts, here is an opportunity to fly around the solar system—and you won't even need a spacesuit! Just will yourself to the planet of your choice and let NASA eat its heart out.

MEETING FRIENDS

Whenever you meet anyone out-of-body—whether people you currently know, people who have passed away, or strangers—it's important to understand that things are not always what they seem. The person you think you are encountering may be your own creation or a hallucinated version. Or a teacher may be assuming the form of someone familiar to you in order to better communicate. On the other hand, the person you think you are encountering may very well be present. Learning to tell the difference is a matter of practice and trusting your intuition. If you sense that the person you communicated with was really there, then trust yourself.

There are several ways to go about meeting friends while out-of-body. One is to do it on your own, in which case you simply try to project yourself to a friend's house. Think of your friend and will yourself to her. You may even wind up meeting your friend in her dream state, and if you are lucky, she may remember the encounter. Or you may wind up at the location of your friend's physical body. A few people have reported being able to see or detect someone else's double, or astral, body. You can try telling your friend to expect you at a certain time in order to increase the possibility of this rather difficult feat.

Another interesting approach to this is for two people to try to meet while out-of-body. Recruit a friend to work with you on this project. You may want to begin by simply using suggestions prior to sleep. On an agreed-upon evening, each of you gives yourself the suggestion that you are going to seek each other out and meet. If you are persistent, you may succeed in meeting during sleep, conversing, and remembering the same experience.

Another method requires both you and your friend to have developed some proficiency in inducing OOBEs. The idea here is to try to induce an OOBE at exactly the same time and then meet somewhere in physical reality. For example, you both agree to wake up at 4:00 A.M., suggest you are going to meet at a specified physical location, and attempt to leave your body at precisely 4:15 A.M.

ASTRAL SEX

Sex outside the body certainly rates as an enjoyable option when considering what to do. Orgasms during lucid dreams or OOBEs can be particularly intense. As already stated, out-of-body experiences can feel as real as physical reality, and that applies to sex as well. Finding a willing partner in the inner worlds generally is no problem. You may find that the self you are while out of body seems somewhat more spontaneous than usual. With regard to moral issues like whether sex outside the body constitutes a form of infidel-

ity, I'll have to take the Fifth Amendment. If you're attached, don't be surprised if your partner isn't thrilled to hear about your non-physical romantic adventures.

VIEWING TARGETS

Have a friend or family member set up a target somewhere in your home prior to your OOBE attempt. For example, he or she can tape a picture from a magazine on a closet door. Open the closet door without looking at the picture just prior to your OOBE. When you induce your OOBE, try to float over to your closet and view the picture.

Another way of trying this is to have a friend set up a target in his or her home so that while out of your body you can visit there and attempt to see it. There are many possible variations on this theme.

These are only a handful of the virtually

limitless things to do once you find yourself outside of your physical body. You undoubtedly will come up with many more as you progress. In the next chapter, we will discuss out-of-body adventures that explore reincarnation and the mysteries of time.

12
REINCARNATION AND TIME TRAVEL

Physicists have been telling us for a while that our concepts about the nature of time need to be revised. It seems the concepts with which we have been raised may bear little resemblance to what really makes the universe tick.

In accordance with Einstein's theories, if one identical twin takes a round-trip space flight at sufficiently high speeds, on his return he will be younger than his sibling. Twenty years may have passed for the twin who stayed on Earth. To the twin who traveled through space at speeds close to the speed of light, however, less time will have passed. There seem to be states or places in which time runs more slowly than normal.

Those interested in the concept of reincarnation usually think of it within the normally accepted framework of time. In other words, it is generally thought that lives are lived consecutively, one after the other. For example, the soul or self may have taken on a body and identity in, say, 1750 and then gone on to its next life in 1850. If our concepts of time are distorted, however, so may be our theories of reincarnation. Lives may not be lived consecutively at all.

According to Robert Monroe, author of *Journeys Out of the Body*, time as we normally think of it does not exist in the nonphysical dimensions to which we often travel while out-of-body. Monroe states that in these dimensions "there is a sequence of events, a past and a future, but no cyclical separation. Both continue to exist coterminously with 'now.' "[1]

My former teacher Seth was in accord with this view of time, only he taught that this is the true nature of time for physical as well as nonphysical reality. Seth used the term *simultaneous time* to explain that the past, present, and future all exist simultaneously in the *now*. This theory has some interesting ramifications. For example, this would mean that all of our reincarnational lives are lived at once. Thus, theoretically it becomes possible to not only remember other lives but visit them, since these lives are still going on.

Whatever your views, if you are interested in exploring reincarnation and the nature of time, the out-of-body experience offers considerable opportunity along these lines. In some out-of-body states, it seems you have access to a certain mobility through time that can result in some startling adventures.

Here's an example of a memorable experience I had. Before I went to sleep I had given myself the suggestion that I would receive some reincarnational information. I believe that some of the reincarnational personalities I met in the following experience were in their dream states when I encountered them:

I found myself in an amusement park waiting in line for one of the attractions. It was a time machine that really worked, and I was amazed and excited as I waited for my turn. Several of my friends were there with me. As I rounded the corner near the booth at the entrance to the time machine, I saw two signs. One said classical and the other said jazz. I thought we were being given a choice of music to listen to, and I chose classical. When my turn came, I went rushing through the portal and immediately found myself flying around in a chamber. At this point, I realized I was out-of-body and got even more excited. I felt totally clear, alert, and full of energy. I turned to my friend and told him that I knew for sure we were out-of-body because I did it all the time and it felt the same. My friend wanted to stay in the chamber, but I wanted to move on. I opened the door and went into the next room. There I saw a classical piano player hard at work. In fact, he was decidedly unfriendly, so absorbed in his work that he didn't take the time to talk to me. I decided to move on and walked through a door. In the next room there was a huge, burly sailor who looked like a pirate. He was sitting with his feet up on a table and a beer in his hand, looking very relaxed and comfortable. He was boisterous and in a booming voice said his name was Charles Anson and that he was involved in the takeover of the Panama Canal. After talking for a short while, I moved on to the next room.

In the next room, I met someone who I now know to be one Henry de Lorraine, Duke de Guise, from sixteenth-century France. At the time, I didn't know his name, noting only that he was an aristocratic gentleman from Old France or England. What really seemed weird to me, though, was that he was apparently frightened of me. He was so frightened, in fact, that he was standing on a chair, where he seemed to feel more comfortable. We spoke. He seemed to think I was some sort of sor-

cerer, and he wanted me to prove it. I thought this was all great fun, and I put my hands out in front of me, made a gesture, and materialized an electric lamp on a nearby table. The lamp, which I materialized with the lights on, did not seem to calm him. On the contrary, he seemed to get more and more upset and indicated to me that he wanted me to make it disappear. So I did. He didn't seem to want to have much more to do with me, so our meeting ended shortly thereafter.

Next, I walked through a door, but instead of finding myself in another room, I was outside in a wooded setting. It was all incredibly vivid, and it felt good to be outside. Suddenly I saw a large mountain man walking toward me. He seemed quite at home in the wilderness. We approached each other until we were standing very close. He knew that I was out of my body. We said hello to each other and smiled. Somehow I recognized this *person. I knew him, but I couldn't remember his name. It was a warm reunion nevertheless, and we embraced.*

When I woke up, I immediately went to the encyclopedia to see whether I could find anything on Charles Anson. I knew little, if anything, about the history of Panama. I could find nothing on Charles Anson, but I did discover that there is a city named Ancon in Panama. It is located in the Canal Zone, right near Panama City, at the mouth of the canal in the Gulf of Panama. And the entire area, it seems, was once the scene of piratical activity. I wondered if perhaps I had heard of the city of Ancon in grade school or somewhere else. I couldn't remember anything of the sort, however.

A reincarnational experience has a certain quality to it that you can recognize with practice. This is an intuitive recognition. In the above experience, a prior suggestion was used, and the time machine made the situation fairly obvious. On other occasions, I have had spontaneous experiences in the dream state that I sensed were reincarnational. In some of these I was another person, and in others I simply found myself observing another time period.

Here is another example of an OOBE with a reincarnational theme from Carl, a participant in my workshops whose OOBEs were mentioned in prior chapters. Carl had given himself a suggestion to get some reincarnational information:

I was lying in bed. I lifted up out of my body in my bedroom [from the hypnagogic state] and decided that I wanted to go somewhere. I had been reading a book about reincarnation, so I had the subject on my mind. I went up through the roof of my building and then somehow wound up above a city. As I looked down, I realized that each of the different houses and blocks represented different time periods. I knew that no matter which one I chose to go to, I would experience something different. At first it was hard for me to go through the roof of one of these houses. I realized that I was having trouble because I was afraid of going back in time and experiencing the past. I decided that if I didn't like what I saw, I could always just pop back to my physical body. So I concentrated on going through the roof, and I slipped right through.

It seemed that I was now in Denmark and it was a long, long time ago. As soon as I went through the roof, I became another person. I was a woman, and I was wearing an old peasant dress. I was walking down a cobblestone street and carrying a basket. It scared me a little, being a different person and everything. I returned to my physical body.

What is the value of such experiences? That depends a lot on your belief systems. For example, the aristocratic gentleman I met in my aforementioned experience has given me some exciting opportunities to explore the subjective meaning of reincarnation. From many sources over time, I have received much information about this particular reincarnational self. I have also received information leading me to believe that some of his contemporaries are now my contemporaries. I can sense his aliveness even now as a portion of my whole self that is connected to me yet is not me. We are both independent identities; yet there are exchanges of energy and information going on, and opportunities to help each other. I think my conscious awareness of the connection between me and my aristocratic friend has somehow amplified communications that naturally occur, on other levels, all the time. I have enhanced the relationship that already existed between us, and it has enriched my life.

The "coincidental" connection mentioned earlier between the name Charles Anson and the Panamanian city Ancon is nothing compared to some of the evidential cases already published. For those seeking something more concrete in terms of evidential material to support theories of reincarnation, much work has already been done by serious researchers. Ian Stevenson, M.D., who has published several books that include cases extremely suggestive of reincarnation, has collected over 2,000 cases to date, most of which are "solved."[2] A "solved" case means that the "past person" that someone claims to have been was traced and identified.

In a recent discussion I had with James Matlock, librarian and archivist at the American Society for Psychical Research (A.S.P.R.), he explained to me that the best cases to support reincarnation were "child" cases. Mr. Matlock lectured on the subject at the Foundation for Research on the Nature of Man, in July 1987, and there described the typical child case as follows:

A child, usually between ages 2 and 5, begins to speak about a previous life. He may say he was so-and-so, lived in such-and-such a place, was married to this person, died in that way. He may talk about the previous life and demand so often to be taken to the place of that life that finally his parents oblige. Quite often, what the child has been saying checks out upon investigation. Moreover, on traveling to the town of the previous life, the child may find his way unaided to the previous home. Once there, he may recognize people and things and ask about others. . . . These [the child cases] are clearly superior to all other types of cases. Not only do the children often give abundant verified details about the previous life or lives they remember, there are aspects of the cases that go well beyond the informational. The children typically exhibit behaviors that are unusual in their families but are consistent with the behaviors of the previous person they are talking about. The behaviors may include strong likes and dislikes, such as in styles of dress and food preferences, and they may include skills of various sorts. . . . Nor is this all. There may be <u>physical</u> correspondences between the subject and the person whose life he claims to remember. These physical correspondences range from general likenesses—about the eyes, the stature, color of skin or hair, and so on—to a subject's birthmarks and congenital deformities. The birthmarks typically resemble in size, shape and position, marks, scars or wounds—typically death wounds—of the previous persons. Thus a child who remembers the life of a person who died by a blow to the head may have a birthmark on the head. . . . It is characteristic of the children cases that they involve previous lives only a few years before and in the same geographical region as the present life. . . . With the other types of reincarnation case, the lengths and distances of intermission are usually much longer. . . .

Children cases have been reported and continue to be reported from various parts of the world, including Europe and the United States. It is a fact, however, that the great majority of cases—and far more of the better cases—develop in places such as India where belief in reincarnation is strong. . . . There is too much data, from too many cases, too consistent with the idea of reincarnation and inconsistent with any other idea for any rival hypothesis really to stand a chance.[3]

Proving reincarnation within the current scientific framework is an extremely difficult affair. No matter how accurately someone describes a past life that checks out, it can always be ascribed to some sort of telepathy or clairvoyance. If, however, you are willing to open your mind, experiment a little, and trust your own intuitive knowledge, you can get your own evidence.

My basic goal in all of this work is learning how to access direct-knowing experiences. Therefore, I am not overly concerned about trying to prove the validity of the concept of reincarnation. Based on my own knowledge, both inner and outer, I choose to believe in reincarnation, and I use it as a working hypothesis. However, I do feel that the full dimensions of what is really involved is pretty mind boggling. I believe we are all evolving into larger beings capable of keeping track of all of our different selves while still retaining the integrity of our identity. Right now we are part of a Greater Self that is already doing this. Someday we will grow into the same position. Learning to wake up to other parts of our beings now is a beginning toward becoming what we will become.

We have all lived many lives. We have only begun to understand the nature of our own identities. The integrity of the unique self we think we are will always be nurtured and preserved—and yet we are all really multiselves. For those interested in exploring these matters firsthand, here are some exercises to play with.

Exercise 6: Meeting Reincarnational Selves

Procedure: When you induce or otherwise find yourself out-of-body, tell yourself you are going to visit a past reincarnational self. Focus on traveling backward in time. If you know of a specific reincarnational self you want to visit, think of that self, visualize it in your mind, and will yourself there. Concentrate your attention as clearly as you can on what you are trying to accomplish. If you prefer, you can visit a future self instead of a past one.

Another way to try this is to simply give yourself a suggestion just prior to going to sleep (for example, "I am going to have a dream in which I receive reincarnational information"). Or try giving yourself the suggestion in a relaxed but alert waking state, in a place where you can sit or lie down undisturbed. Simply quiet your mind and be open to whatever impressions you receive.

Exercise 7: Traveling Through Time

Procedure: When you induce or otherwise find yourself in the out-of-body state, tell yourself you are going to travel to your own city in the year 1850 or if you prefer, 2150 (or any time or location you want to visit)

Say to yourself out-loud and while out of your body, "I am now traveling backward (or forward) in time." Concentrate your attention and feel yourself moving to your desired destination.

A simpler version of this is to give yourself the same suggestions just prior to sleep (for example, "I am going to have a dream in which I visit England in the seventeenth century.").

Exercise 8: Visiting Your Childhood Self

This exercise can be done from either an out-of-body state or relaxed waking state, as presented here.

Procedure: Sit or lie down in a quiet, dark place. Close your eyes and take a few long, slow, deep breaths. With each exhalation, tell yourself that your body is relaxing. Quiet your mind. Let go of thoughts and worries. Think about yourself as a child. Pick an approximate age you liked, and imagine that childhood version of yourself is still alive in the eternal now. See your childhood self in your mind. Try to sense the feeling of that child's existence. Tell yourself several times that your childhood self is alive right now. Then imagine that you are traveling backward in time to visit your childhood self. As vividly as you can, imagine that you have arrived and are now with your childhood self.

Communicate whatever you wish. Perhaps give support or reassurance of what is to come or simply be with your childhood self and allow him or her to remind you of the wisdom of play and spontaneity. When you are finished, say goodbye for now and imagine yourself returning to your own time. Tell yourself to return, and in your mind see yourself back in the present. When you are back,

open your eyes and take some time to focus yourself clearly in the present moment.

Exercise 9: Meeting an Older You

As with Exercise 8, you can try this exercise from an out-of-body state or from a relaxed waking state, as presented here. This exercise will require a little background material. The future is malleable. Therefore, whatever future version of yourself you tune into is only one of a number of possible futures available to you. According to Seth, all of these probable versions of yourself actually exist, each in its own probable world. In other words, there are parallel selves and parallel universes. Seth calls these *probable selves*. To simplify: If you really wanted to be a surgeon and you also really wanted to be a dancer, both versions of you exist. According to your beliefs, thoughts, and emotions you become one of these probable selves. The other probable selves are no less real, and they exist in their own dimensions. I mention this concept here because it is important to realize that the future is never cast in stone. Whatever version of yourself you tune into with the following exercise is not necessarily the one you eventually will become. It is one version of yourself that you *can* become. Remember: Since you create your reality, you can change the course of your future at any point by altering your thoughts and beliefs in the present. I refer those interested in more information about probable selves to *Seth Speaks*[4] and *The Unknown Reality*,[5] both written by Jane Roberts.

Given the above, you can use the following exercise to visit a future self that is a natural outgrowth of the current version of yourself.

Procedure: Proceed the same way as in Exercise 8, but this time hold in your mind the idea of an older version of yourself—at age eighty-five or any other age you like. Keep in mind that this self is now alive in its own time, and begin to sense the feeling of this self as vividly as you can. Imagine yourself moving forward in time until you reach this older version of yourself. Just be with your older self for awhile, and feel what you are feeling. Speak to your older self. Perhaps you want to ask this older version of yourself for some general or specific advice. When you are finished, say goodbye and tell yourself to return to your own time. Imagine and feel yourself coming back to the present. When you have returned, open your eyes and take some time to focus yourself clearly in the present moment.

Exercise 10: Experiencing the Eternal Now

Procedure: Just before going to sleep, lie

quietly and relax your mind. Tell yourself that the future and the past are happening now. Imagine that everything that is going to happen has already happened, and yet, paradoxically, brand new events continue to emerge. Imagine that the entire history of the universe is still happening. Try to engage your intuitive knowledge as you mentally play with this concept. Try to feel it. Then, as you are settling down to sleep, give yourself the suggestion that you are going to have an OOBE that will help you understand the nature of time.

A FINAL NOTE

The excitement and freedom so often associated with OOBEs are really intrinsic elements of our being. Our very existence is exciting, and freedom to create what we want in our lives is our natural state.

Working with OOBEs is not meant to replace or supersede our experience in physical reality. Right now we are physical beings. It is true that right now we are also nonphysical beings, but even so, we are now physical beings. The current opportunity before us involves our fulfillment as physical creatures. Our current challenge is the artful materialization of love, creativity, and understanding in our physical lives.

Many have allowed themselves to lose sight of their own magic and importance in the universe. If your OOBEs help remind you how utterly magnificent it is to be alive in the physical universe, you are using them well.

Happy Flying!

Although I may be unable to write back to everyone, I would love to hear about your out-of-body experiences and which techniques work best for you. I also offer audiocassette programs and metaphysical workshops in various cities. For further information, you can write me at the following address:

Rick Stack
P.O. Box 1506
Gracie Station
New York, NY 10028

NOTES

Chapter 1

1. Oliver Fox, *Astral Projection: A Record of Out-of-the-Body Experiences* (Secaucus, N.J.: Citadel Press, 1962), pp. 56–60.
2. K. Osis and D. McCormick, "Kinetic Effects at the Ostensible Location of an Out of Body Projection during Perceptual Testing." *Journal of the American Society for Psychical Research* 74 (1980): pp. 319–329.
3. R. Morris, S. Harary, J. Janis, J. Hartwell, and W. G. Roll, "Studies of Communication During Out of Body Experiences." *Journal of the American Society for Psychical Research* 72 (1978): pp. 1–21.
4. Fox, *Astral Projection*, p. 47.
5. Richard Bach, *The Bridge Across Forever* (New York, William Morrow & Co., Inc., 1984) pp. 376–379.

Chapter 2

1. S. Blackmore, *Beyond the Body* (London: Paladin Grafton Books, 1983), pp. 82–93. Reprinted 1986. Originally published in Great Britain by William Heinemann Ltd., 1982.
2. K. Ring, *Life at Death* (New York: Coward, McCann & Geoghegan, 1980), p. 45.

Chapter 3

1. José Silva, *The Silva Mind Control Method* (New York: Simon and Schuster, 1977), p.61.

2. Napoleon Hill, *Think and Grow Rich* (New York: Fawcett World Library, 1960), p. 50.
3. Jane Roberts, *The Nature of Personal Reality: A Seth Book* (Englewood Cliffs, N.J.: Prentice-Hall, 1974).

Chapter 4

1. Jane Roberts, *The Nature of Personal Reality: A Seth Book* (Englewood Cliffs, N.J.: Prentice-Hall, 1974), p. 65.

Chapter 5

1. Jane Roberts, *The Seth Material* (Englewood Cliffs, N.J.: Prentice-Hall, 1970), pp. 177–179.
2. Jane Roberts, *Seth, Dreams and Projection of Consciousness* (Walpole, N.H.: Stillpoint Publishing, 1986), pp. 315–348.

Chapter 9

1. Robert Monroe, *Journeys Out of the Body* (Garden City, N.Y.: Anchor Press/Doubleday, 1977) pp. 73–76.

Chapter 10

1. Paul Tholey, "Techniques for Inducing and Maintaining Lucid Dreams," *Perceptual and Motor Skills 57* (1983): pp. 79–90.
2. Stephen Laberge, *Lucid Dreaming* (Los Angeles: Jeremy P. Tarcher Inc., 1985). p. 149.
3. Ibid., p. 155.

Chapter 12

1. Robert Monroe, *Journeys Out of the Body* (Garden City, N.Y.: Anchor Press/Doubleday, 1977), p. 74.
2. J. G. Matlock, "Reincarnation" (Lecture read at the Foundation for Research on the Nature of Man, Durham, N.C., July 1987).
3. Ibid.
4. Jane Roberts, *Seth Speaks: The Eternal Validity of the Soul* (Englewood Cliffs, N.J.: Prentice-Hall, 1972).
5. Jane Roberts, *The "Unknown" Reality: A Seth Book*, vol. 1 (Englewood Cliffs, N.J.: Prentice-Hall, 1977).

BIBLIOGRAPHY

Bach, Richard. *The Bridge Across Forever.* New York: William Morrow & Co. Inc, 1984.

Blackmore, Susan. *Beyond the Body.* London: Paladin Grafton Books, 1983. Reprinted 1986. Originally published in Great Britain by William Heinemann Ltd., 1982.

Crookall, Robert. *The Study and Practice of Astral Projection.* Secaucus, N.J.: Citadel Press, 1960.

Fox, Oliver. *Astral Projection: A Record of Out-of-the-Body Experiences.* Secaucus, N.J.: Citadel Press, 1962. Copyright 1962 by University Books, Inc.

Garfield, Patricia. *Creative Dreaming.* New York: Ballantine Books, 1976 (paperback); New York: Simon & Schuster, 1974 (hardcover).

Gawain, Shakti. *Creative Visualization.* Mill Valley, Cal.: Whatever Publishing, 1978.

Gershon, David, and Gail Straub. *Empowerment; The Art of Creating Your Life as You Want It to Be.* New York: Dell, forthcoming 1989.

Green, Celia. *Out of the Body Experiences.* New York: Ballantine Books, 1973.

Laberge, Stephen. *Lucid Dreaming.* Los Angeles: Jeremy P. Tarcher Inc., 1985.

Mitchell, Janet Lee. *Out-of-Body Experiences: A Handbook*. New York: Ballantine Books, 1987 (paperback); Jefferson, N.C.: McFarland & Co., 1981 (hardcover).

Monroe, Robert. *Journeys Out of the Body*. Garden City, N.Y.: Anchor Press/Doubleday, 1977. Originally published by Doubleday & Company, 1971.

Muldoon, Sylvan, and Hereward Carrington. *The Projection of the Astral Body*. New York: Samuel Weiser, 1970. Originally published by Rider & Co., 1929.

Perl, Sheri. *Healing from the Inside Out*. New York: New American Library, forthcoming 1989.

Ring, K. *Life at Death*. New York: Coward, McCann & Geoghegan, 1980.

Roberts, Jane. *The Seth Material*. Englewood Cliffs, N.J.: Prentice-Hall, 1970.

Roberts, Jane. *Seth Speaks: The Eternal Validity of the Soul*. Englewood Cliffs, N.J.: Prentice-Hall, 1972.

Roberts, Jane. *The Nature of Personal Reality: A Seth Book*. Englewood Cliffs, N.J.: Prentice-Hall, 1974.

Roberts, Jane. *The "Unknown" Reality: A Seth Book*, vol. 1. Englewood Cliffs, N.J.: Prentice-Hall, 1977.

Roberts, Jane. *The "Unknown" Reality: A Seth Book*, vol. 2. Englewood Cliffs, N.J.: Prentice-Hall, 1979.

Roberts, Jane. *The Nature of the Psyche: Its Human Expression: A Seth Book*. Englewood Cliffs, N.J.: Prentice- Hall, 1979.

Roberts, Jane. *The Individual and the Nature of Mass Events: A Seth Book*. Englewood Cliffs, N.J.: Prentice- Hall, 1981.

Roberts, Jane. *A Seth Book: Dreams, "Evolution," and Value Fulfillment*, vol. 1. Englewood Cliffs, N.J.: Prentice-Hall, 1986.

Roberts, Jane. *A Seth Book: Dreams, "Evolution," and Value Fulfillment*, vol. 2. Englewood Cliffs, N.J.: Prentice-Hall, 1986.

Roberts, Jane. *Seth, Dreams and Projection of Consciousness*. Walpole, N.H.: Stillpoint Publishing, 1986.

Rogo, D. Scott. *Leaving the Body*. Englewood Cliffs, N.J.: Prentice-Hall, 1983.

Silva, José. The Silva Mind Control Method. New York: Simon and Schuster, 1977.

Targ, Russell, and Keith Harary. *The Mind Race*. New York: Ballantine Books, 1985.